Where to watch birds in

Tenerife

©2000 Publicaciones Turquesa S.L.
Apartado de Correos 686
38080 Santa Cruz de Tenerife
Canary Islands
Spain
Tel: (00 34) 922 24 79 61

© Text and maps: Eduardo García del Rey
© Photos: Eduardo García del Rey, Pedro F. Acosta (nº 3, 4, 5 & 6 pag. 143), Sixto Cozzi
(nº 1 pag. 146), José Manuel Moreno (nº 3 & 4 pag. 15, pag. 16, nº 2 pag. 57, nº 2 pag. 71,
nº 4 pag. 108, nº 1, 2 pag. 116 & nº 1 pag. 127), Fernando Cova (nº 1, 2, pag. 15 & nº 1 pag. 107)
© Illustrations: José Manuel Moreno

Designed: Publicaciones Turquesa/ Alberto García del Rey
Layout designer: Alberto García del Rey
Cover photograph: José Manuel Moreno
Typeset: Fotomecánica Contacto
Depósito legal: TF:365/2000
ISBN: 84-95412-07-1
Printed in Spain

Where to watch birds in

Tenerife

Eduardo García del Rey

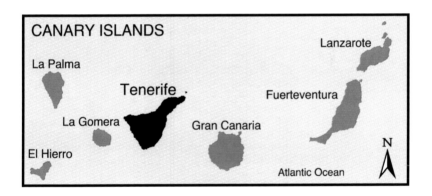

Ilustrations by
José Manuel Moreno

CONTENTS

ACKNOWLEDGMENTS

I am grateful to my parents and my brother and sister for all their support, and especially grateful to my future wife, Eva, for her companionship and patience in the field while visiting many of the sites mentioned in this guide.

I am also extremely grateful to the Canarian Ornithological Community, who has helped me in a variety of ways over the past eight years. In particular, I would like to thank Dr Juan Jose Bacallado Aránega, Dr Aurelio Martín, Jose Manuel Moreno (editor and illustrator), Guillermo Delgado, Ruben Barone, Juan José Ramos, Manuel Siverio, Juan Antonio Lorenzo, Barry Lancaster and Keith Emmerson for their kindness, assistance and advice.

MAP OF THE MACARONESIAN REGION

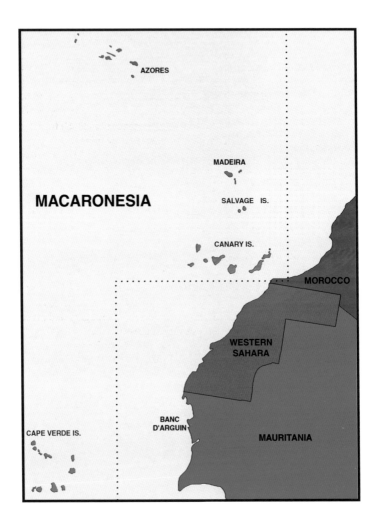

FOREWORD

The Canary Islands, of which Tenerife is the largest, are remarkable. Lying off the coast of Morocco and, at their nearest point less than 100 km from the African mainland, the Canaries have frequently been referred to as the European Galapagos. However, despite comparison with that famous archipelago, where Charles Darwin gained such important insight into the process of biological evolution, the use made of the Canaries by biologists remains well below their potential. The seven main islands of the Canaries offer a diverse range of habitats from lush Laurel forests on the western islands, strongly influeced by the Atlantic, to true desert conditions on the eastern islands, swept by easterly winds from the Sahara. As is admirably described in this book,Tenerife alone offers a wide range of habitats, owing especially to the great height of Mount Teide. It is no wonder then that these islands have provided opportunities for the evolution of numerous endemic forms from the unique and extraordinary radiation of numerous species of *Euphorbia*, to the Blue Chaffinch which breeds in the vicinity of Mount Teide itself.

Despite the importance of the islands to biologists, the birdwatcher in the Canaries is poorly served by existing fieldguides. This seems to be because books on the birds of Europe regard the Canaries as too remote or too African to include thoroughly, while works on the birds of Africa consider them too European. The truth is of course that they are both. Their avifauna is derived as much from Europe, as for example the Blue Tit, Chaffinch and Robin, as from North Africa, for example the sandgrouse and Houbara on Fueteventura. But the common European birds are all uniquely distinct. The Blue Tits of the Canaries may be so different now from the nearest continental forms that they might be recognised as a distict species, indeed perhaps more than one distinct species, the different forms of Chaffinches bear testiment to multiple invasions in prehistoric times, and the Robin, which differs somewat in appearance from its European ancestor, sings a unique song.

So the Canaries offer much for the birdwatcher, ornithologist and evolutionary biologist alike. All of them will benefit from this remarkable book, which I am certain, will also help to promote the unique biological treasures of the Canaries in general, and Tenerife in particular. Eduardo Garcia del Rey has done a great service for all of us in researching the material for this book so thoroughly and presenting it in such an accessible form. It deserves every success.

Dr Andrew G Gosler FLS
Edward Grey Institute of Field Ornithology,
University of Oxford

BIRDWATCHING TENERIFE

Tenerife is the largest and highest of all the Canary Islands, and birdwatching Tenerife can be extremely rewarding due to its range of ecosystems, which are more numerous and varied than those of the other seven islands. All the endemics, except Canary Islands Chat (only found on Fuerteventura), can be observed on Tenerife. Berthelot´s Pipit, Canary Islands Chiffchaff and Canary occur in a wide range of habitats and can be located easily. Blue Chaffinch, however, is only to be found in the pine forests although it is easier to see here than on Gran Canaria, and the two endemic pigeons, Bolle´s Pigeon and Laurel Pigeon, can be found in the last remaining patches of laurel forest and its surroundings. Canary Islands Kinglet is abundant, but being so tiny, it can sometimes be very hard to spot. Plain Swift is the only Macaronesian endemic that partially migrates to North Africa for the winter, but it can still be found on Tenerife in this season, only in smaller numbers.

A few Eastern Canaries specialities inhabit Tenerife. The South still holds small populations of Stone-curlew, Barbary Partridge, Lesser Short-toed Lark and Trumpeter Finch. Barbary Falcon can be reliably found on Tenerife, along with Rock Sparrow, but unfortunately Red Kites and Egyptian Vultures are completely extinct from the island.

Tenerife occupies a central position in the Canary Islands, and the ferry crossings to Gomera (27 km/17 miles) and Gran Canaria (60 km/37 miles) provide excellent opportunities for observing seabird species such as Bulwer´s Petrel, Little Shearwater, Cory´s Shearwater and European Storm-petrel. From Tenerife it is also easy to reach the Salvage Archipelago, which lies 114 km/70 miles to the northwest of the Canaries and offers the best opportunity in the Western Palearctic to see White-faced Storm-petrel.

A further interesting fact is that Tenerife has the highest number of local birders in the Canaries, all of whom contribute regularly to the knowledge and understanding of the resident and migrant avifauna. It is thanks to their dedication that Tenerife boasts the largest number of migrant bird species recorded in the Archipelago.

ECOLOGICAL ZONES AND HABITATS

Tenerife has four main ecological zones (ecosystems):

Lower zone:

- Islets, and coastal cliffs.
- Rocky coasts, sandy beaches and sand dunes.
- Euphorbia scrub (Cardonal-tabaibal).
- Urban and cultivated areas, golf courses, ponds and reservoirs.

Laurel forest zone:

- Fayal-brezal.

Pine forest zone.

High mountain zone (Teide National Park).

LAUREL FOREST

PINE FOREST

HIGH MOUNTAIN ZONE

LOWER ZONE

Offshore islet

Coastal cliff

Sandy beach

Euphorbia scrub (Cardonal-tabaibal)

Pond

Reservoir

LOWER ZONE:

Islets and coastal cliffs:

There are two small islets, Roques de Anaga, off the northeastern coast of Tenerife, and one islet to the north of the island, near Garachico. All three are isolated and fully protected, which makes them ideal habitats for colonies of seabirds like Bulwer´s Petrel, Cory´s Shearwater, Little Shearwater, European Storm-petrel, Madeiran Storm-petrel and Yellow-legged Gull.

The massive, virtually inaccessible cliffs in the Teno and Anaga regions hold a few pairs of Barbary Falcon and Osprey.

Rocky coasts, sandy beaches and sand dunes:

Tenerife´s rugged, rocky coastline attracts a fair number of wintering visitors and the occasional migrant, the most representative species being Little Egret, Ringed Plover, Grey Plover, Whimbrel, Common Sandpiper, Turnstone and Sandwich Tern.

There are also numerous coves around the island, with small beaches of black volcanic sand, and near San Andrés in the northwest, there is an artificial beach with pale sand from the Sahara. As most of the beaches are generally overcrowded, very few birds can be observed on them. However, Sanderling is the most representative during the winter months.

Unfortunately today, Médano is the only place in Tenerife where it is possible to see coastal sand dunes. This unique, fragile habitat is composed of salt-tolerant plants (halophytic).

Euphorbia scrub (Cardonal-tabaibal):

This is considered to be the original habitat of the lower zone, and is dominated by shrubs and endemic *euphorbias*, succulent plants which thrive in arid conditions, and which are very similar to the cacti of the Americas. The most representative flora in the Euphorbia scrub is Balo (*Ploclama pendula*), Cardón (*Euphorbia canariensis*), Tabaiba dulce (*Euphorbia balsamifera*), Tabaiba amarilla (*Euphorbia regis-jubae*). In addition, this habitat is the year round home to Stone-curlew, Lesser Short-toed Lark, Berthelot´s Pipit, Spectacled Warbler, Southern Grey Shrike and Trumpeter Finch.

Urban and cultivated areas, golf courses, ponds and reservoirs:

As the human population grows, Tenerife´s urban areas are expanding, and this has led to an increase in the number of Spanish Sparrows and some introduced birds, such as Ring-necked Parakeet, Monk Parakeet and Common Myna, all of which now have well-established populations on the island.

There are a few grasslands or cultivated fields in Tenerife where Linnet and Corn Bunting breed, and which are sometimes used as wintering grounds by some European migrants; Lapwing, Short-eared Owl, European Golden Plover, Stonechat, etc.

Golf courses have become very popular in Tenerife over the last decade, and they act as magnets for birds, attracting all kinds of migrants.

The man-made ponds and reservoirs, which provide the water for the island's irrigation system are also breeding grounds for Moorhen, Coot and Little Ringed Plover.

LAUREL FOREST ZONE:

The laurel forest, often shrouded in thick cloud, is an evergreen forest that overhangs the ridges in a dramatic way as a result of its constant exposure to the strong trade winds from the north. It can only be found in the northern and north-eastern regions of the island, at altitudes of between 500 and 1000 metres with a very high rainfall. The forest is dominated by fifteen species of tree, which belong to ten different families; four of them belonging to the laurel family. The most representative species are Laurel (*Larus azorica*), Barbusano (*Apollonias barbujana*), Viñatigo (*Persea indica*), Til (*Ocotea foetens*), Acebiño (*Ilex canariensis*), Palo blanco (*Picconia excelsa*).

The laurel forest is home to the elusive Woodcock and the two species of endemic pigeon, Bolle's and Laurel Pigeon. Manx Shearwater breeds here in small numbers.

Fayal-brezal:

This habitat lies at altitudes of 1000-1500 metres, and is dominated by two small trees; Faya (*Myrica faya*) and the heath Brezo (*Erica arborea*), from which this ecosystem gets its name. Canary Islands Kinglet frequents this type of tree although it is also used by other passerines such as Blackbird, Chaffinch, etc.

PINE FOREST ZONE:

The pine forest is composed of Canary Pine (*Pinus canariensis*) and found at altitudes of between 1200 and 2000 metres in the North, and from 500 metres upwards in the South. Very few plant species are able to survive in this forest, but it is quite easy to see clusters of Faya (*Myrica faya*) or Brezo (*Erica arborea*) in the North, and Adenocarpus (*Adenocarpus foliolosus*) in the South. Blue Chaffinch and Great Spotted Woodpecker are only found in this type of forest.

HIGH MOUNTAIN ZONE:

This region encompasses Teide National Park and the surrounding mountains. It begins above the pine forest at an altitude of about 1900 metres and is dominated by plants that are very well adapted to extreme conditions: Retama (*Spartocytisus supranubius*) and Codeso (*Adenocarpus viscosus*). Avifauna found in this zone includes Berthelot's Pipit, Canary Islands Chiffchaff and Southern Grey Shrike.

WHERE TO LOOK FOR MIGRANTS ON TENERIFE

Migration is mainly dependent on weather conditions. However, species that are in transit over large bodies of water are attracted by Tenerife´s landscape and the golf courses and reservoirs, which provide welcome food and shelter.

Although migrants can turn up in virtually any of the ecosystems, they tend to congregate in the lower zone, where they wait for the right conditions to continue their journey. Some birds search the island for suitable habitats, and some even decide that Tenerife is their last stop.

Migrants are also easier to detect in the lower zone as there are fewer resident bird species here, and the availability of suitable habitats is limited.

In order to increase the probability of finding a rare migrant, it is a good idea to concentrate on certain areas at certain times of the year.

Migrants come from four different regions: North America, Asia, Africa and Europe.

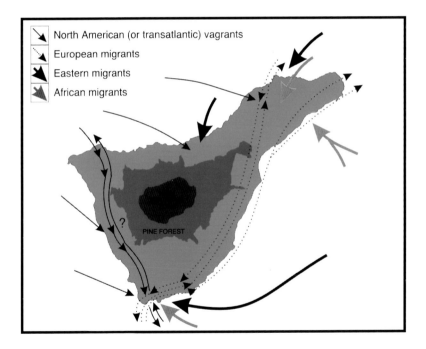

MAP 1: MIGRATION THROUGH TENERIFE

This map shows the possible patterns of migration through Tenerife proposed by the author. Wind direction is represented by the arrows, which will help you decide when to visit a site, and thus increase your chances of finding a rare bird.

North American (or tansatlantic) vagrants

Between September and November many North American birds migrate from the northeastern regions of the continent to South America. During the long voyage, they are sometimes driven off-course and blown towards Europe by strong westerly winds. Some drown in the Atlantic while others, if they can, land on ships. Only a small percentage of those that set out survive to reach Tenerife. From the higher number of ducks, waders and gulls recorded, it can be deduced that larger birds have a better chance of survival than do smaller birds. Ring-necked Duck, Lesser Scaup, Spotted Sandpiper, Pectoral Sandpiper, Buff-breasted Sandpiper, White-rumped Sandpiper, Lesser Yellowlegs, Baird´s Sandpiper, American Golden Plover and Ring-billed Gull are the most frequent North American vagrants to Tenerife. The best time to look for these is autumn, from September until the end of November. Birds that winter on the island do not normally stay longer than mid March/beginning of April.

Asiatic vagrants

Many North Asiatic bird species that winter in South Asia also make long migratory journeys. However, only a very small number migrate west to Tenerife. The reasons for this are not yet fully understood, but it has been put down to either an internal (genetic) or an external (magnetic anomalies in the area of hatching) factor in their navigational sense. The few that have been recorded on Tenerife are Pallid Harrier, White-tailed Plover, Richard´s Pipit, Yellow-browed Warbler, Red-breasted Flycatcher and Rose-coloured Starling.

Unfortunately, a great number of potential Asiatic migrants are imported to Tenerife every year for commercial purposes, thus decreasing the probability of true vagrancy. Autumn is a good time to look for these although February is perhaps the best month.

African vagrants

Some African bird species undertake weather-related movements. Presumably in the dry season they migrate to areas where they can find water and are caught by strong southerly winds that push them towards the Canary Islands and Tenerife. Some bird species that have reached Tenerife in this way include; Allen´s Gallinule, Little Swift, Blue-cheeked Bee-eater and Desert Wheatear.

Although they are very unpredictable, African migrant species are easiest to spot during December, February and June.

European migrants

These include passing migrants and wintering birds. Some passing European migrants are regularly recorded in passage while others have become rarer on Tenerife during migration. Autumn migration (post-nuptial migration) starts in August and ends in December, reaching a peak in October/November whereas Spring migration (pre-nuptial) begins in February and ends in June, reaching a peak in March/April. The most frequently recorded European migrants include; Purple Heron, Curlew Sandpiper, Dunlin, Ruff, Common Redshank, Swallow, House Martin, Yellow Wagtail (various races), Northern Wheatear, Chiffchaff (various races), Willow Warbler, Spotted Flycatcher, Pied Flycatcher, Woodchat Shrike.
Passing seabird migration starts in August and ends in November with representative

species such as, Great Shearwater, Manx Shearwater, Leach´s Storm-petrel, Grey Phalarope, Great Skua and Pomarine Skua.

Some birds visit Tenerife every winter while others only from time to time. The most frequently recorded are various kinds of ducks, waders, gulls, terns and few passerines: Wigeon, Gadwall, Common Teal, Pintail, Shoveler, Tufted Duck, Coot, Ringed Plover, European Golden Plover, Grey Plover, Lapwing, Sanderling, Little Stint, Common Snipe, Whimbrel, Greenshank, Green Sandpiper, Common Sandpiper, Turnstone, Black-headed Gull, Lesser Black-backed Gull, Sandwich Tern, Meadow Pipit, Red-throated Pipit, White Wagtail, Black Redstart and Song Thrush.

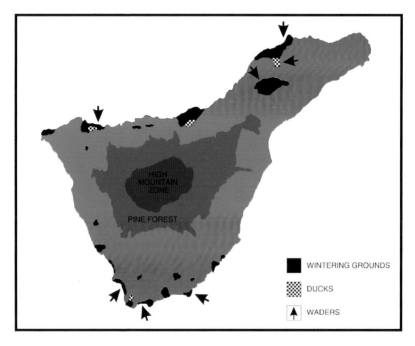

MAP 2: WINTERING SITES
This map will help you decide where to look for winter visitors.

CLIMATE

Generally speaking, Tenerife, like the rest of the Western Canary Islands, has a Mediterranean climate. However, there are five factors which influence the island's weather conditions and prevent the climate from being completely uniform:

1) Geographical Latitude: Tenerife is located about 500 km/300 miles north of the Tropic of Cancer, which makes it a subtropical oceanic island. Such islands normally enjoy relatively mild winters and cool summers.

2) Altitude: As the altitude increases, the climate changes drastically. From sea level to about 750 metres the temperatures are hot and there is little rainfall. In the North, between 750 metres and 1500 metres a constant sea of cloud makes the air extremely damp and humid. This cloud is formed when a cool mist, brought in by the northeasterly trade winds, rises and condenses as it comes into contact with the island's warm slopes. The laurel forest and fayal-brezal thrive in these climatic conditions. From 1500 metres upwards, the weather is more continental with extreme temperatures and low rainfall. The dominant winds are from the northwest and are less humid.

Above 2000 metres, Tenerife offers a subalpine climate with cool southwesterly winds. In winter, there is snow.

3) Canary Current: This cold sea current prevents the island from getting too hot in the summer and helps maintain a relatively mild temperature.

4) Trade Winds: "Los Alisios or tiempo norte". This northeast wind blows for most of the year and creates the cloud of sea in the north of the island. It favours autumn migrants moving south and affects spring migrants moving north.

5) Proximity to North Africa: Locally known as "siroco" or "tiempo sur", this south-eastly wind from the Sahara fills the air with dust, "calima", which hangs over the island for a few days although it can stay for weeks. These are perfect weather conditions for spotting African vagrants.

PRE-TOUR INFORMATION

Entering the Canary Islands

The Canary Islands belong to Spain, and the entry requirements are exactly the same. EU citizens do not need a passport (valid identification will be enough), but non-EU citizens do need a valid passport. No visa is required if staying less than three months.

Currency and exchange rate

The Spanish currency is the "peseta", and as of May 1999, you get 250 Pesetas for one Pound and 150 Pesetas in exchange for one US Dollar. There are numerous hotels and banks where money can be exchanged easily. Visa cards and traveller's checks are also accepted in most places. Remember that in the most remote areas you will have to exchange money in banks, so check the office hours.

Accommodation

Tenerife offers a wide range of accommodation; hotels, apartments, pensions (bed and breakfast). You can contact the tourist office and ask for a brochure with a complete list at:

Excmo. Cabildo Insular de Tenerife.
Oficina de Infomación Turística
Plaza de España, s/n
38003 Santa Cruz de Tenerife.
Tel: (00 34) 922 23 95 92
Fax: (00 34) 922 23 97 81
http://www.cabtfe.es/puntoinfo/texto/E/index.html

Most of the hotels are situated in the south of the island, in Los Cristianos and Las Americas, but there is also plenty of accommodation in Puerto de la Cruz, Los Gigantes and Santa Cruz. Rural tourism is becoming very popular and visitors are beginning to favour this more relaxed style of accommodation. Camping is not a very good option on Tenerife as there are very few official campsites.

Recommended field clothing

Sun hat	Sandals
Windjammer	Lightweight shoes
Swimwear	Lightweight sweater
Sturdy walking boots/ shoes	Lightweight waterproof jacket
Light and medium weight shirts	Shorts

Recommended miscellaneous equipment

Binoculars	Telescope and tripod
Alarm clock	Camera and film
Field guides	Torch and extra batteries
Small rucksack or shoulder bag	Notebook and pencil
Spare binoculars – (in case of loss or damage)	
Spare spectacles – (in case of loss or damage)	

Insurance

Theft is a worldwide problem. If you are bringing expensive optical equipment or other valuable items, please be sure you have adequate insurance. If in doubt, seek the advice of your insurance broker.

Field Guides for birdwatching

Heinzel, H. et all. Collin Pocket Guide: Birds of Britain and Europe with North Africa and Middle East. 1995. This bird guide offers the best value for money and covers all the endemic species and subspecies of the Canary Islands.

Jonsson, L. Birds of Europe: Identification Guide. 1992. Helm, London. All five volumes of the original series in one book, with many new illustrations. One of the best guides on European birds available but will not cover many of the Canarian species and subspecies that you will encounter.

Harrison, P. Seabirds of the World: A Photographic Guide. 1996. Christopher Helm. A compact guide.

Moreno, J.M.1988. Guía de las Aves de las Islas Canarias. Editorial Interinsular Canaria.

TRAVEL

Car hire
It is very easy to rent a car in Tenerife. The regular day price is about 5000 Pesetas or about 20 Pounds per day. You can hire in advance, or on arrival at the airport.

Sea and air
Various fast options are offered for visiting the other islands by sea, but the most convenient from a birdwatcher´s point of view is the traditional slow ferry.

Three companies operate various routes: Fred Olsen, Transmediterranea and Naviera Armas. The Fred Olsen ferry to Gomera leaves Los Cristianos harbour every day at 9:00, 12:30, 16:00 and 20:00. Price per person is about 4000 Pesetas or 16 Pounds return. The return trip from San Sebastian to Cristianos leaves at 7:00, 10:45, 14:15 and 18:00. It is advisable to arrive one hour before departure, especially if you are taking a car with you. There is an additional charge for vehicles.

There are also departures from Los Cristianos to Hierro and La Palma. For more information contact:

Edificio Fred Olsen
Pol. Ind. Añaza s/n
Santa Cruz de Tenerife
Tel: (00 34) 922 62 82 00
Fax: (00 34) 922 62 82 01

Transmediterranea and Naviera Armas operate between Tenerife and Gran Canaria. For updated information contact:

Naviera Armas S.A.	**Transmediterranea**
Dársena Pesquera los Llanos s/n	Edificio Puerto Ciudad
38001 S/C de Tenerife	Muelle Ribera
Tel:(00 34) 922 53 40 52	38001 S/C de Tenerife
Fax:(00 34) 922 28 97 58	Tel:(00 34) 02 45 46 45

The internal airline is operated by **"BINTER Canarias"** and should be booked in advance as they have a limited number of seats. The flight is very short, and there is no food served on board.

If you would like to charter a yacht to sail around the islands or visit the Salvage Archipelago, please contact:

AVES ECOTOURS S.L.
C/ Fdo. Barajas Vilchez 9
38004 Santa Cruz de Tenerife
Canary Islands
Spain.
Tel: (00 34) 922 27 99 58
Tel: (00 34) 922 22 17 50
Fax: (00 34) 922 22 16 69
e-mail: avesecot@redkbs.com

MAPS

Maps can be bought in many different shops around the island.
Santa Cruz de Tenerife 1:200,000 (Spanish National Survey)
Tenerife 1:150,000 (Mairs)
Tenerife 1:150,000 (Daily Telegraph)
Tenerife 1:100,000 (Hildebrand)
V1 Tenerife 1:150,000 (Firestone)
E50 Tenerife 1:150,000 (Firestone) Tenerife only
Spanish Military Topographic Survey 1:200,000/1:100,000/1:50,000

HEALTH

Tenerife is a very safe island to visit. There are no poisonous snakes or plants, and no dangerous wild animals.

The tap water is safe in most parts of the island although it is not advisable to drink it in the South. Bottled water is available in all supermarkets and shops.

There are very good medical facilities near Santa Cruz and Playa de Las Americas.

WHEN TO GO

The endemics can be seen all year round although the rarer Laurel Pigeon is more visible from May to September, and the winter months are not a good period for Plain Swift as it partly migrates to Africa.

If you are interested in migrants and would like to know the best time to look for them, please refer to "Where to look for migrants on Tenerife" (page 17).

If you are looking for seabirds, the best time is mid-May to early September, and there are always a few passing through between August and November. Madeiran Storm-petrel only breeds in winter, arriving at their breeding grounds in the north east of the island in November and departing at the end of the winter season.

In general, the best time is in May. August is also a good time, but the temperatures are at their highest then.

HOW TO USE THIS BOOK

The most important part of this book is the site information guide with the lists of species you can expect to see at each particular site. However, the pre-tour information section is also important as it will help you to plan and prepare for your trip. An introduction to the possible migration patterns through Tenerife has been included to enable you to select the best sites to look for migrants.

REGIONS OF TENERIFE

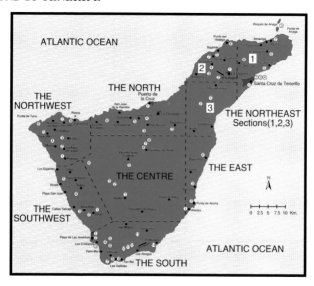

Region chapters

The 68 major sites are grouped by regions, with some regions divided into sections. This book covers the following regions of Tenerife: The South, the Southwest, the Northwest, the North, the Northeast (Section 1, Section 2, Section 3), the East and the Centre.

The regions are briefly outlined in the introduction to each chapter.

Maps

The regional map shows all major birdwatching sites. Most sites have a site map which differ in scale and detail. Key features are noted on the maps.

Key

Sites

The official category of the site is given although most sites are unprotected. If the site has any additional local name, this is also listed.

Information on type of habitat, best time to visit, location, strategy for birdwatching, birds (year round, summer visitors, winter visitors, passage migrants, accidentals and escapes) and other wildlife in the area is given for each site.

Site description

This lists the major habitats and the breeding birds to be seen. Sometimes the site is subdivided into areas, represented by letters (A,B,C,D,E).

Time to visit:

Advice on the best months to visit the site, taking into consideration weather conditions and other relevant factors.

Location:

Directions on how to get to the site are given from the major tourist resorts and cities of Tenerife (Santa Cruz, Las Américas/Los Cristianos, Puerto de la Cruz).

Strategy:

Information on where to park and the best way of approaching the site and the surrounding areas.

Birds:

All species recorded at the site are listed. The status of the species is categorised as one of the following: year round, summer visitors, winter visitors, passage migrants, accidentals and escapes. Species with an asterisk * has been accepted by the Spanish Rarities Committee or have been recorded by the author.

Other wildlife:

Information on additional fauna such as mammals, cetaceans, reptiles and butterflies is given when appropiate.

THE
SOUTH (TFS)

Trumpeter Finch

SITE INFORMATION

THE SOUTH (TFS)

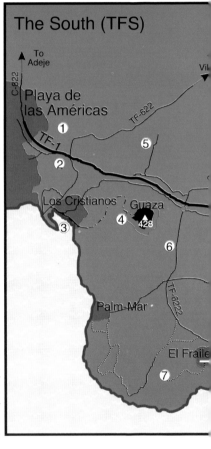

The South (TFS)

The South is characterised by large, flat areas of exposed volcanic rock, covered with volcanic cinders and dust. The coastline is extremely rugged, but there are a few sandy beaches and coastal plains.

The flora is dominated by species of *euphorbia*, succulent cacti-like plants well adapted to dry conditions.

This southern region is a perfect example of Tenerife´s Lower Ecological Zone, and presents a direct contrast to the lower zone in the North, which is now mostly urban or occupied by banana plantations.

This type of habitat found on Tenerife is also present on the eastern islands of Fuerteventura and Lanzarote, and so it is not surprising that the two groups of islands have some bird species in common.

The South of Tenerife, however, has been severely fragmented and disturbed by tourist resorts, banana and tomato plantations and several recently established golf courses. This has led to the increasing scarcity of Barbary Partridge, Stone-curlew, Lesser Short-toed Lark and Trumpeter Finch, all of which are now extremely difficult to find on Tenerife although they remain fairly common on the eastern islands.

Punta de la Rasca (TFS7) and Montaña Roja at El Medano (TFS14) are considered Special Natural Reserves, and Guaza Mountain (TFS4) has been declared a Natural Monument. All are of ornithological importance and are considered "protected areas". We hope they remain so for generations to come.

One positive aspect about the South is that it is extremely attractive to migrant bird species, boasting one of the best sites in the entire Archipelago. El Fraile Reservoir (TFS7) and its surroundings have produced a list of over 90 recorded bird species, many of which have been first time sightings for Tenerife and the Archipelago.

In general, the landscape is poor and at times depressing, but the birdlife definitely makes up for this.

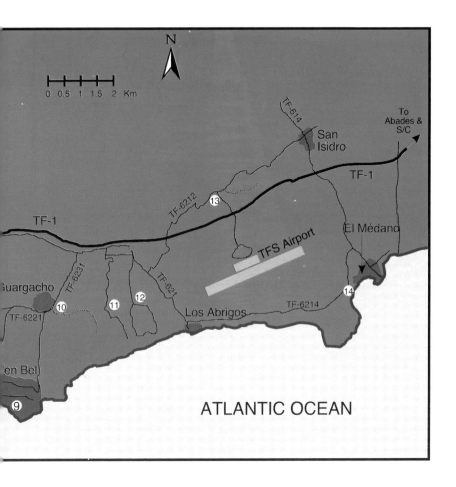

● LAS AMERICAS RESERVOIR   TFS1
Category: none
(Caldera del Rey)

Description:
This small reservoir is located on a prime migratory route for birds moving south.
Although under-watched, it is used by passing migrants, depending on water levels.
Sometimes birds wintering on other reservoirs close-by get attracted here, so it
deserves a quick look.
The three *sylvia* warblers resident to Tenerife can be found in the surroundings of
the reservoir.

Time to visit:
Autumn migration is probably the best time to look for rarities (September-November), and a winter visit might produce a few interesting species. During the summer months it is prone to being dry.

Location:
From Santa Cruz/ Los Cristianos: Take motorway TF-1 to Los Cristianos and exit at San Eugenio and Parque Acuatico (Salida 29). Follow the signs to Parque Acuatico until you see Aquapark Octopus on your left. Turn right at Avenida Europa and go up past BelAir on your right until you reach a dirt track signposted

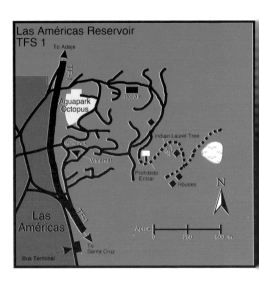

"Prohibido Entrar and Propiedad Privada". Ignore this sign and proceed onto the dirt track. Turn right at the Indian Laurel Tree and follow the road. Make a left at the T-junction by the houses and after 0.5 km you will see the reservoir on your right.

From Las Americas: Follow the signs to Parque Acuatico until you see Aquapark Octopus on your left. Turn right at Avenida Europa and drive up past BelAir on your right until you reach a dirt track signposted "Prohibido Entrar and Propiedad Privada". Ignore this sign and proceed onto the dirt track. Turn right at the Indian Laurel Tree and follow the road. Make a left at the T-junction by the houses and after 0.5 km you will see the reservoir on your right.

Strategy:
The track is in fairly good condition.
Scan the shores of the reservoir with a telescope, looking for birds.

Birds:
Year round: Little Egret, Grey Heron, Yellow-legged Gull, Common Kestrel, Moorhen, Rock Dove, Long-eared Owl, Plain Swift, Hoopoe, Berthelot´s Pipit, Grey Wagtail, Blackbird, Spectacled Warbler, Sardinian Warbler, Blackcap, Canary Islands Chiffchaff.
Summer visitors: Turtle Dove, Pallid Swift.
Passage migrants/ winter visitors: Common Teal, Shoveler, Lapwing, Common Snipe, Greenshank, Swallow, House Martin.

● **LAS AMERICAS GOLF COURSE**   **TFS2**
Category: none

Description:
This golf course was opened in 1998. Like other golf courses in the South, it could become an excellent site for the future as it acts as a magnet for migratory bird species.

Time to visit:
During migration, and especially during autumn migration.

Location:
From Santa Cruz: Take motorway TF-1 to Los Cristianos and exit at Playa de Las Americas (Salida 28). Follow the signs to Campo de Golf Las Americas. Park in the car park.

Strategy:
Walk around the golf course looking out for birds. Beware of golfers and straight shots.

Birds:
Year round: Yellow-legged Gull, Common Kestrel, Little Ringed Plover, Rock Dove, Collared Dove, Plain Swift, Hoopoe, Berthelot´s Pipit, Grey Wagtail, Blackbird, Spectacled Warbler, Blackcap, Canary Islands Chiffchaff, Spanish Sparrow.
Summer visitors: Turtle Dove, Pallid Swift.
Winter visitors: Whimbrel, Lesser Black-backed Gull.

● FERRY TO GOMERA   TFS3
Category: none

Description:
The ferry crossing to Gomera offers a superb opportunity to look for seabirds in the Western Canaries although the best opportunities are obtained by chartering a yacht. Two companies cover this route, Transmediterranea and Fred Olsen. The latter is the one most birdwatchers use as it offers extra height and better visibility.

Time to visit:
The majority of seabirds are present from May to September although Cory´s Shearwater can arrive as early as February and depart as late as November. Passing seabird migrants occur from August to November. (Madeiran Storm-petrel arrives at Roques de Anaga (TFNE13) in late September, or early October to breed during the winter months).

Location:
From Santa Cruz: Take motorway TF-1 to the Los Cristianos exit (Salida 72). At the traffic lights, turn right and follow the signs to "Puerto". Turn left into the valet parking area, or park in the area.

Strategy:
If you are planning to take your vehicle with you to Gomera, it is advisable to arrive at the harbour one hour before departure.
Stand as close to the bow as possible and view the sea from the highest point. To increase the probability of successful sightings stay on the left side of the boat on both the outward and return trips. It is best to catch the latest ferry available as seabirds are coming ashore to rest at this time.

Birds:
Year round: Little Shearwater, Yellow-legged Gull.
Summer visitors: Bulwer´s Petrel, Cory´s Shearwater, Manx Shearwater, European Storm-petrel, Common Tern.

Winter species: Madeiran Storm-petrel, Gannet, Grey Phalarope, Great Skua, Lesser Black-backed Gull*, Kittiwake*, Sandwich Tern*.

Passage migrants: Great Shearwater*, Manx Shearwater*, Gannet*, Grey Phalarope*, Pomarine Skua*, Arctic Skua*, Long-tailed Skua*, Great Skua*, Lesser Black-backed Gull.

Accidentals: Fea´s/Zino´s Petrel, Sooty Shearwater, Wilson´s Storm-petrel, White-faced Storm-petrel, Leach´s Storm-petrel*, Red-billed Tropicbird*, Roseate Tern, Sooty Tern.

(Winter species, passage migrants and accidental birds with an asterisk * have been accepted by the Spanish Rarities Committee, or have been recorded by the author).

Other wildlife:

Fish: Tropical Two-winged Flyingfish (*Exocoetus volitans*), Oceanic Two-winged Flyingfish (*Exocoetus obtusirostris*), Bennett´s Flyingfish (*Cypselurus pinnatibarbatus*).

Reptiles: Loggerhead Turtle.

Cetaceans: Sperm Whale, Bryde´s Whale, Fin Whale, Cuvier´s Beaked Whale, Killer Whale, Short-finned Pilot Whale, Bottlenose Dolphin, Spotted Dolphin, Striped Dolphin, Common Dolphin, Rough-toothed Dolphin.

● GUAZA MOUNTAIN   TFS4
Category: Natural Monument
(Montaña de Guaza)

Description:
The Guaza Mountain National Monument is a semi-desert area, dominated by *euphorbia* plants (cacti-like) and can be considered as the last stronghold on Tenerife of the rare Trumpeter Finch. This area has been relatively untouched by man and offers the visitor a superb opportunity to explore one of the last natural refuges in the south.

Time to visit:
The best time to visit is during the spring and summer months as birds are breeding and generally more active. A winter visit can also be rewarding if you are looking for Trumpeter Finch. To avoid the high temperatures that usually hit this area it is advisable to visit either early in the morning or towards the end of the afternoon.

Location:
From Santa Cruz/ Las Americas: Take motorway TF-1 to the Los Cristianos exit (Salida 72). At the traffic lights turn left. (Do not follow "centro ciudad"). Take the first right to Avenida de los Crisitianos. Follow the road to the end, passing the Gran Hotel Arona until you get to Urbanizacion Bameco (Parque Tropical). Park anywhere that looks safe.

Strategy:
Just near the stoney beach there is a trail signposted "Montaña de Guaza", which leads to the plateau. Follow the green dots painted on the rocks until you get to the plateau. It is about a 30 or 45-minute walk, so make sure you have plenty of water and suncream to combat the hot sun.

If you are visiting this site during migratory periods, it is worth taking a quick look

around the tamarisks for passerine migrants.
Look for waders near the coast in winter.
Try to reach the plateau early in the morning
and walk around to locate the Trumpeter
Finch via its call, which sounds like a
miniature toy trumpet. There are not many
species in this area, so check any bird that
you see flying in the vicinity.

Birds:
Year round: Little Egret, Common Kestrel,
Stone-curlew, Yellow-legged Gull, Rock
Dove, Collared Dove, Barbary Dove, Monk
Parakeet, Long-eared Owl, Plain Swift,
Hoopoe, Berthelot´s Pipit, Spectacled

Trumpeter Finch

Warbler, Canary Islands Chiffchaff, Southern Grey Shirke, Spanish Sparrow,
Trumpeter Finch.
Summer visitors: Common Tern, Turtle Dove, Pallid Swift.
Winter visitors: Cattle Egret, Grey Plover, Whimbrel, Common Sandpiper,
Turnstone, Mediterranean Gull, Black-headed Gull, Audouin´s Gull, Lesser Black-
backed Gull, Sandwich Tern.
Passage migrants: Cattle Egret, Spoonbill, Oystercatcher, Northern Wheatear.

Other wildlife:
Canary Lizard, Rabbit, Short-finned Pilot Whale.

● CACTUS PARK RESERVOIR   TFS5
Category: none
(Presa Llano Azul)

Description:
This small reservoir with very little vegetation is strategically located to attract any
bird moving south. Although under-watched, it is worth a quick look during
migration. During the summer months it is prone to being dry.

Time to visit:
During the months of September to November, or February to June. A winter visit
could be rewarding.

Location:
From Santa Cruz: Take the motorway TF-1 to Los Cristianos and exit on Valle San
Lorenzo (Salida 26). Turn left by the sign "KM 5" or "Centro Hípico del Sur" and
follow this road for 1.5 km. Take the first right-hand turn and after 0.8 km, park
near the houses on your right. Walk towards los Cristianos, or towards the stoney
walls. The reservoir is behind these walls.

From Las Americas/ Los Cristianos: Take motorway TF-1 to Santa Cruz and exit
on Valle San Lorenzo/Las Galletas (Salida 26). At the roundabout, turn right to
Valle San Lorenzo. Pass the tunnel and turn left at the sign "KM 5" or "Centro
Hípico del Sur". Follow this road for 1.5 km. Take the first right and after 0.8 km,
park near the houses on your right. Walk towards los Cristianos, or towards the
stoney walls. The reservoir is behind these walls.

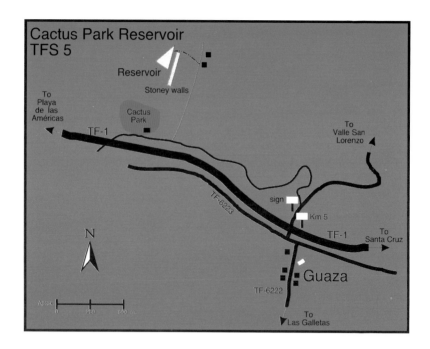

Strategy:
It is recommended that you approach slowly and not expose yourself too much as birds might be flushed by your presence.
Scan the shores of the reservoir with a telescope to look for birds.

Birds:
Year round: Little Egret, Grey Heron, Common Kestrel, Barbary Partridge, Moorhen, Yellow-legged Gull, Rock Dove, Long-eared Owl, Plain Swift, Hoopoe, Berthelot´s Pipit, Grey Wagtail, Spectacled Warbler, Spanish Sparrow.
Summer visitors: Turtle Dove.
Winter visitors: Greenshank, Common Sandpiper.

● LOS PALOS GOLF COURSE   TFS6
Category: none

Description:
This is a very small golf course in the semi-desert scrub, so it attracts migrants and some resident bird species.

Time to visit:
To avoid high temperatures, it is advisable to visit either early in the morning or towards late afternoon. Best time during migration.

Location:
From Santa Cruz: Take motorway TF-1 to the Las Galletas exit (Salida 26). Pass the tunnel and turn left. Turn right at the roundabout and drive through Guaza. The Golf Course is on your right.

From Las Americas/ Los Cristianos: Take motorway TF-1 to the Las Galletas exit (Salida 26). Go straight over at the roundabout and pass through Guaza. The Golf Course is on your right.

Strategy:
Follow the big screen all the way to the southern tip, keeping an eye out for straight shots.

Birds:
Year round: Little Egret, Common Kestrel, Little Ringed Plover, Yellow-legged Gull, Rock Dove, Long-eared Owl, Plain Swift, Hoopoe, Berthelot´s Pipit, Grey Wagtail, Blackbird, Spectacled Warbler, Canary Islands Chiffchaff, Southern Grey Shrike, Spanish Sparrow.
Summer species: Turtle Dove, Pallid Swift.
Winter visitors: Cattle Egret, Whimbrel, White Wagtail.
Passage migrants: Cattle Egret, Ruff, Sand Martin, Skylark, Swallow, House Martin, Red-throated Pipit, Blue-headed Wagtail, Yellow Wagtail, Whinchat, Northern Wheatear.

● EL FRAILE RESERVOIR & PUNTA DE LA RASCA   TFS7

Category:
El Fraile Reservoir: none
Punta de la Rasca: Special Nature Reserve
Other names:
El Fraile Reservoir: Embalse de Salema, Roquito del Fraile, Charca Bonny
Punta de la Rasca: Malpaís de Rasca, Punta Rasca

Description:
This is an area of low hills and flat land, with clumps of *euphorbia* and low scrub, a few banana and tomato plantations and some abandoned fields to the north. It gets very little rain, and it is normally very hot and sometimes windy.
The area is famous for El Fraile Reservoir (A), the largest reservoir in southern Tenerife . Punta de la Rasca (B) is the last remaining coastal patch of desert-scrub, and there is an excellent place near the lighthouse for seawatching. To the North, there are some Abandoned fields (D), with a few Indian Laurel trees (C). These trees used to be a regular site for Long-eared Owl, and it is still a good spot for migrants.

Time to visit:
The best time to visit the reservoir to look for non-resident birds is between September and June. The best time for seawatching is from February to September.

Location:
From Santa Cruz: Take motorway TF-1 to the Las Galletas exit (Salida 26). Pass the tunnel and turn left. Turn right at the roundabout and drive through Guaza. Pass Golf Los Palos and go straight over at the roundabout. You will see the track to the Abandoned fields (D) on your right near the second banana plantation, just before the petrol station. If you are going to the Reservoir (A), pass the petrol station and take the second turn on your right to the village of El Fraile. Follow the street all the way to the end. Turn left and take the first right by the football pitch. After passing some houses on the left, turn right onto the track. Follow the track to the end and park near the red and white gate.

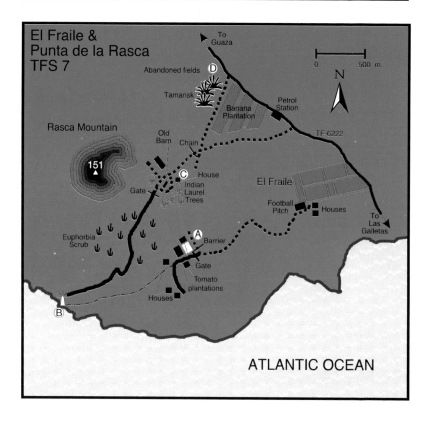

El Fraile &
Punta de la Rasca
TFS 7

To Guaza

Abandoned fields (D)

0   500 m.

N

Tamarisk

Petrol Station

Banana Plantation

Rasca Mountain

Old Barn   Chain

TF-6222

151

House

Gate

(C)

Indian Laurel Trees

El Fraile

Football Pitch

Houses

To Las Galletas

Euphorbia Scrub

(A)

Barrier

Gate

Tomato plantations

Houses

(B)

ATLANTIC OCEAN

From Las Americas/ Los Cristianos: Take the motorway TF-1 to the Las Galletas exit (Salida 26). Go straight over at the roundabout and pass through Guaza. Continue on past Golf Los Palos and once again go straight over the roundabout. You will see the track to the Abandoned fields (D) on your right near the second banana plantation, just before the petrol station. If you are going to the Reservoir (A), pass the petrol station and take the second turn on the right to El Fraile. Follow the street all the way to the end. Turn left and take the first right by the football pitch. Go pass some houses and then turn right onto the track. Follow the track to the end and park near the red and white gate.

Strategy:
To view the Reservoir (A), look through the holes in the concrete wall. A telescope is very useful although a bit difficult to use. If this is not successful, the other option is to look through the blue door on the north side of the reservoir. For seawatching at Punta de la Rasca (B) a telescope is essential.

(A) El Fraile Reservoir:
In addition to being the largest reservoir in southern Tenerife, El Fraile is also well located to attract a good number of migrant bird species. It is surrounded by a 3-metre high concrete wall and holds water all year round. This is probably why it is the only breeding site for Coot in Tenerife. Ducks can be seen during the winter

months, and Trumpeter Finch also visits the reservoir occasionally to drink. Sometimes resident and migratory Ospreys and resident Barbary Falcon appear in autumn and winter. A visit to this site during winter and migration (September-June) is a must for any birdwatcher.

The access track is in good condition, and suitable for any type of vehicle.

(B) Punta de la Rasca:

This is a protected area of coastal *euphorbia* scrub. It used to be good for Barbary Partridge, Lesser Short-toed Lark and Trumpeter Finch, but all these bird species are now extremely scarce. Plain Swift, Berthelot´s Pipit, Southern Grey Shrike and Spectacled Warbler can be seen from the access road to the Lighthouse (B). The Lighthouse is considered to be one of the best seawatching headlands on Tenerife, and even Bulwer´s Petrel and Little Shearwater have been seen from here. Cory´s Shearwater and Short-finned Pilot Whale are easier to observe.

There are two ways to get to the Lighthouse. The easiest way is from the El Fraile Reservoir (A), and it takes about 30 minutes (2.5 km) each way from the locked gate at the northern end. From the Reservoir, cross the red and white metal gate and follow the road. Immediately after the road bears left, there is a trail that leads to the Lighthouse. If the workers stop you, tell them that you are visiting the Lighthouse, "El Faro" in Spanish.

(C) The Indian Laurel trees:

These planted trees have provided a sheltered roosting place for breeding Long-eared Owl. In more recent years, it has become a less popular site, possibly due to the high number of visitors to this area, or the deteriorating condition of the trees. From time to time, you can see the odd Osprey on the telephone poles near the trees. It is important to be as quiet as possible when approaching these trees and to keep your visit brief so as not to disturb any owls that could be roosting. A good time to visit this habitat is at dusk or during the night as this is when Stone-curlews and the occasional Long-eared Owl can be heard calling. To get to this area, follow the tracks southwest of TF-6222.

(D) Abandoned Fields:

This is one of the last natural breeding sites for Stone-curlew on Tenerife, and its future existence is uncertain as new banana plantations are being established in the area. The Aulaga (*Launaea arborescens*) dominates the landscape and this is an excellent place for Southern Grey Shrike, which can sometimes be seen perched on the clumps of cacti-like plants (*Euphorbia canariensis*). Alpine Swift and Red-rumped Swallow have also been recorded passing through this area, and Black Redstart has be known to winter here.

Birds:

Year round: Little Shearwater, Little Egret, Grey Heron, Osprey, Common Kestrel, Barbary Falcon, Barbary Partridge, Moorhen, Coot, Stone-curlew, Little Ringed Plover, Yellow-legged Gull, Rock Dove, Collared Dove, Long-eared Owl, Plain Swift, Hoopoe, Lesser Short-toed Lark, Berthelot´s Pipit, Grey Wagtail, Spectacled Warbler, Canary Islands Chiffchaff, Southern Grey Shrike, Spanish Sparrow, Trumpeter Finch.

Summer visitors: Bulwer´s Petrel, Cory´s Sheartwater, Turtle Dove, Pallid Swift.

Winter visitors: Spoonbill, Wigeon, Gadwall, Common Teal, Mallard, Pintail, Garganey, Shoveler, Pochard, Tufted Duck, Ringed Plover, Grey Plover, Lapwing, Little Stint, Dunlin, Black-tailed Godwit, Spotted Redshank, Common Redshank,

Greenshank, Common Sandpiper, Turnstone, Black-headed Gull, Lesser Black-backed Gull, White Wagtail, Black Redstart.

Passage migrants: Black-necked Grebe*, Gannet*, Cormorant*, Squacco Heron*, Cattle Egret, White Stork, Garganey*, Shoveler*, Black Kite*, Marsh Harrier, Hen Harrier, Montagu´s Harrier, Osprey*, Peregrine Falcon, Quail, Black-winged Stilt*, Avocet*, Collared Pratincole, Lapwing*, Knot*, Little Stint, Temminck´s Stint, Curlew Sandpiper*, Dunlin, Ruff*, Common Snipe*, Black-tailed Godwit*, Whimbrel, Spotted Redshank*, Common Redshank*, Whiskered Tern, Black Tern, Common Swift*, Alpine Swift*, European Bee-eater, Skylark, Sand Martin*, Swallow*, Red-rumped Swallow*, House Martin*, Tawny Pipit*, Tree Pipit, Red-throated Pipit, Yellow Wagtail*, Common Redstart*, Northern Wheatear*, Black-eared Wheatear, Olivaceous Warbler, Subalpine Warbler, Orphean Warbler, Willow Warbler, Spotted Flycatcher, Pied Flycatcher, Woodchat Shrike, Serin.

Accidentals: Great White Egret, Glossy Ibis, Greater Flamingo*, White-fronted Goose, Greylag Goose, Brent Goose, Green-winged Teal, Ring-necked Duck*, Lesser Scaup*, Eleonora´s Falcon, American Golden Plover*, Baird´s Sandpiper*, Pectoral Sandpiper, Buff-breasted Sandpiper*, Long-billed Dowitcher, Spotted Sandpiper*, Little Gull, Sabine´s Gull, Common Gull, White-rumped Swift, Little Swift, Desert Wheatear, Snow Bunting.
(Passage migrants and accidental birds with an asterisk * have been accepted by the Spanish Rarities Committee or have been recorded by the author)

● LAS GALLETAS   TFS8
Category: none

Description:
This used to be a quiet fishing village, but has grown with the tourist industry. The harbour is of little interest to birdwatchers, but the sandy beach and coastal lava reef to the east are good for waders and terns. In strong winds Cory´s Shearwater can sometimes be seen from here. There are a number of bars and restaurants from where it is possible to enjoy the birdlife.

Time to visit:
This site is worth visiting in the winter months and during low tide.

Location:
From Santa Cruz: Take motorway TF-1 to the Las Galletas exit (Salida 26). Pass the tunnel and turn left. Turn right at the roundabout and drive through Guaza. You pass the Los Palos Golf Course on the right and go straight over at the second roundabout. Follow the road until you reach Las Galletas. Park anywhere on the main street near the harbour.

From Las Americas/ Los Cristianos: Take the motorway TF-1 to the Las Galletas exit (Salida 26). Go straight over the roundabout and pass through Guaza. You pass the Los Palos Golf Course on your right and then go straight over at the second roundabout. Follow the road until you reach Las Galletas. Park anywhere on the main street near the harbour.

Strategy:
Walk along the beach towards the rocky area (intertidal zone), which is only exposed at low tide. At high tide there are only a few rocks visible. Check for terns and waders in the area. A telescope is essential for seawatching and can help in locating wintering waders.

Birds:
Year round: Little Egret, Yellow-legged Gull, Plain Swift, Spanish Sparrow.
Summer visitors: Cory´s Shearwater.
Winter visitors: Ringed Plover, Grey Plover, Whimbrel, Common Sandpiper, Turnstone, Mediterranean Gull, Black-headed Gull, Sandwich Tern.
Passage migrants: Collared Pratincole*, Whimbrel*.
Accidentals: American Golden Plover, Spotted Sandpiper*.
(Passage migrants and accidental birds with an asterisk * have been accepted by the Spanish Rarities Committee or have been recorded by the author)

Other wildlife: Bottlenose Dolphin.

● TEN-BEL   TFS9
Category: none

Description:
Ten-Bel, which stands for Tenerife-Belgium, is a tourist resort with private complexes and offers the only artificially grown woodland in the south of Tenerife. These trees attract a fairly good number of migrants, some decide to winter here, but the majority just pass through. The best area is the small park, where there are a few eucalyptus trees, several pines and some low bushes, although migrants can turn up virtually anywhere.
Ten-Bel is one of the best sites in Tenerife to see Plain Swift during the winter months and especially around dusk when they come down to roost near the coast. Barbary Dove, which has been breeding feral, can be considered a speciality for this area although it is in danger of being displaced by the dominant Collared Dove. Sometimes escapes from other parts of the south get attracted to Ten-Bel, so do not be surprised if you see a Common Myna from Asia, a Saphron Finch from Venezuela, or even a Cut-throat Finch from Africa.

Time to visit:
The best time is during migration and the winter months between September and June. Stormy weather from the Sahara, known locally as "tiempo sur" (with dust in the air), with east or southeast winds is excellent for migrants moving north and for African vagrants.

Location:
From Santa Cruz: Take the motorway TF-1 to the San Miguel exit (Salida 72). Follow the signs to Las Galletas. 0.8 km after the sign to Amarilla Golf Course turn left to Las Galletas and Costa del Silencio (TF-6231). Follow the road through Guargacho and to Las Galletas. Turn left to enter Ten-Bel just before you reach the coast (or Las Galletas). The park (or plaza) is on your right. Park anywhere safe.

From Las Americas/ Los Cristianos: Take the motorway TF-1 to the Las Galletas exit (Salida 26). Go straight over at the roundabout and pass through Guaza. Go past Golf Los Palos and straight over at the second roundabout. Follow the road past El Fraile on the left until you reach Las Galletas. Drive all the way to the end of Las Galletas and turn left onto a major road. Once on this road, be ready to make a right hand turn into Ten-Bel. You will see the park and the plaza on your right. Park anywhere near this area.

Strategy:
Walk around the main plaza and look for migrants in the trees. During the winter months wait for the Plain Swifts to fly overhead in late afternoon.

Birds:
Year round: Sparrowhawk, Common Kestrel, Yellow-legged Gull, Rock Dove, Barbary Dove, Collared Dove, Ring-necked Parakeet, Plain Swift, Hoopoe, Grey Wagtail, Blackbird, Spectacled Warbler, Blackcap, Canary Islands Chiffchaff, Blue Tit, Common Myna, Spanish Sparrow.
Summer visitors: Turtle Dove, Pallid Swift.
Winter visitors: Whimbrel, Starling.
Passage migrants: European Bee-eater, Sand Martin, Swallow*, House Martin, Tree Pipit*, Yellow Wagtail*, Song Thrush*, Reed Warbler*, Subalpine Warbler*, Chiffchaff sp.*, Willow Warbler*, Spotted Flycatcher*, Pied Flycatcher*, Woodchat Shrike, Serin.
Accidentals: Merlin*, Blue-cheeked Bee-eater, Red-breasted Flycatcher*.
Escapes: Hill Myna, Common Myna, Purple Glossy Starling, Saphron Finch, Cut-throat Finch, Yellow-fronted Canary, Peach-faced Lovebird.
(Passage migrants and accidental birds with an asterisk * have been accepted by the Spanish Rarities Committee, or have been recorded by the author).

● GUARGACHO TFS10
Category: none

Description:
From an ornithologist's point of view, the three reservoirs (A) are what make this small town interesting. They are very accessible, but unfortunately, have recieved little water for the past few years.
Another attraction for the birdwatcher is the plains (B) to the east of the town, which are considered to be the most reliable site in Tenerife for the rare Lesser Short-toed Lark (*polatzeki* race).
If there is enough rain in winter, larks will use it as their breeding grounds in spring.

Time to visit:
It is worth checking the reservoirs (A) during migration to see if the water level is good, but spring is the best time to look for Lesser Short-toed Lark on the plains (B).

Location:
From Santa Cruz: Take motorway TF-1 to the San Miguel exit (Salida 72). Follow

Lesser Short-toed Lark
(polatzeki ssp.)

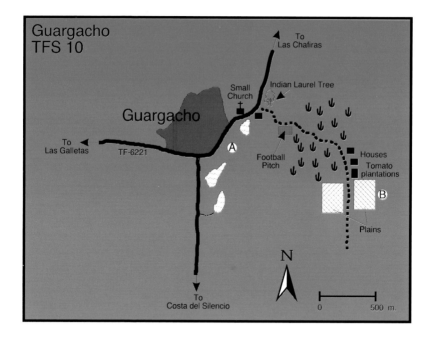

the signs to Las Galletas. 0.8 km after the sign to Amarilla Golf Course, turn left to Las Galletas and Costa del Silencio (TF-6231). You will see Guargacho on your right and the first reservoir on your left. Park near the small church.

From Las Americas/ Los Cristianos: Take motorway TF-1 to the Las Galletas exit (Salida 26). Turn left at the roundabout and follow this secondary road until you reach the sign to Las Galletas and Costa del Silencio (TF-6231). Turn right and keep on this road until you reach Guargacho on your right. You will see the reservoir on your left. Park near the small church.

Strategy:
The dirt track to the plains (B) is in good condition. Look up towards the sky and listen for larks. If you do not spot them fairly quickly, walk around the fields. If you still cannot see them, it is possible that they have decided not to breed in the area.

Birds:
Year round: Little Egret, Common Kestrel, Stone-curlew, Little Ringed Plover, Rock Dove, Plain Swift, Hoopoe, Lesser Short-toed Lark, Berthelot´s Pipit, Grey Wagtail, Spectacled Warbler, Southern Grey Shrike, Spanish Sparrow.
Summer visitors: Turtle Dove, Pallid Swift.
Passage migrants: Night Heron, Cattle Egret, Purple Heron, Spoonbill, Spotted Crake, Little Crake, Baillon´s Crake, Black-winged Stilt, Little Stint, Curlew Sandpiper, Black-tailed Godwit, Common Swift, Short-toed Lark, Swallow, Red-rumped Swallow, House Martin, Tawny Pipit, Tree Pipit, Bluethroat, Woodchat Shrike.
Accidentals: Glossy Ibis, Shelduck, Blue-winged Teal, Marsh Sandpiper.

● AMARILLA GOLF COURSE   TFS11
Category: none

Description:
This golf course is located in an area of semi-desert scrub and is an excellent place
to look for migrants. In the past years Red-throated Pipit has used the stoney plains,
(D) and abandoned fields (B) as wintering grounds. Lesser Short-toed Lark can
sometimes be seen in these same areas. The *euphorbia* scrub on either side of the
road is good for Stone-curlew although this species is difficult to find.
The reservoir (A) just before the security post is a very good site for Little Egret
and also attracts the occasional migrant. Unfortunately, a new road has been built
near the reservoir, which could decrease the potential of this site.
The smaller pools (C) can be surprisingly rewarding, and they deserve a quick
look.

Time to visit:
Any visit during migratory periods could be productive (September to November)
and (February to June). Winter can also be rewarding.

Location:
From Santa Cruz/ Las Americas/ Los Cristianos: Take motorway TF-1 to the San
Miguel exit (Salida 72). Follow the sign to Las Galletas. Turn left at "Amarilla
Golf Course and Country Club". You can see the reservoir from the road. Park in
the lay-by on your right. If you want to visit the other areas, follow the road down
towards the coast and park in the club house car park.

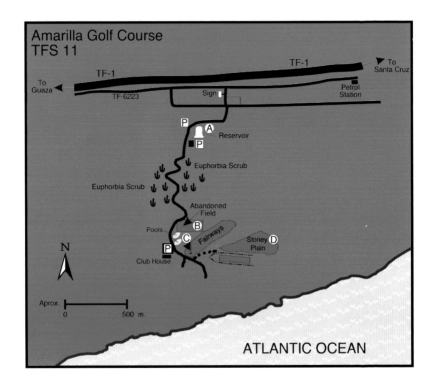

Strategy:
Despite major road construction in this area, these birding sites might be still accessible in the future. Walk around the edges of the golf course, but remember not to obstruct golfers, who have priority at all times. Try not to cross the fairways as this can upset them.

Birds:
Year round: Little Egret, Grey Heron, Common Kestrel, Barbary Falcon, Stone-curlew, Little Ringed Plover, Yellow-legged Gull, Rock Dove, Plain Swift, Hoopoe, Lesser Short-toed Lark, Berthelot´s Pipit, Grey Wagtail, Spectacled Warbler, Southern Grey Shrike, Spanish Sparrow.
Summer visitors: Turtle Dove, Pallid Swift.
Winter visitors: Cattle Egret, Whimbrel, Greenshank, Common Sandpiper, Black-headed Gull, Meadow Pipit, Red-throated Pipit, White Wagtail, Starling.
Passage migrants: Night Heron*, Spoonbill*, Black-winged Stilt*, Cream-coloured Courser*, Collared Pratincole*, Dotterel*, Lapwing*, Little Stint*, Dunlin*, Ruff*, Common Snipe*, Common Redshank*, Wood Sandpiper*, European Bee-eater, Short-toed Lark*, Skylark, Sand Martin*, Swallow*, House Martin*, Tawny Pipit*, Tree Pipit*, Red-throated Pipit*, Blue-headed Wagtail*, Yellow Wagtail*, Common Redstart*, Whinchat*, Northern Wheatear*, Subalpine Warbler, Chiffchaff sp.*, Willow Warbler*, Spotted Flycatcher*, Woodchat Shrike*.
Accidentals: Glossy Ibis, American Golden Plover, White-rumped Sandpiper, Baird´s Sandpiper, Buff-breasted Sandpiper*, Aquatic Warbler.
Escapes: Namaqua Dove, Yellow-crowned Bishop, Monk Parakeet.
(Passage migrants and accidental birds with an asterisk * have been accepted by the Spanish Rarities Committee, or have been recorded by the author.)

● GOLF DEL SUR & CIGUAÑA RESERVOIR   TFS12
Category: none

Description:
This golf course (B & C) has proven to be as productive as Amarilla Golf Course and is another must for the birdwatcher looking for migrants. Ciguaña Reservoir (D) used to be an excellent site until it dried up. Hopefully the dam will be repaired soon so that it will be able to maintain a water supply.
The speciality of this area is Stone-curlew, which can be found fairly regularly on the plains (A) to the north of the club house. A good number of migrants have been recorded in or near the small reservoir (B) on the course although the water levels are unpredictable as it is used for irrigation. The lower levels seem to be the most attractive to migrant birds.

Time to visit:
The best time to visit is during migration (September to November or February to June).

Location:
From Santa Cruz/ Las Americas/ Los Cristianos: Take motorway TF-1 the Los Abrigos exit. Follow the signs to Los Abrigos and Golf del Sur. Park near the reservoir or at the club house.
To get to Ciguaña Reservoir (D) follow the road to Los Abrigos. Immediately after the stoney street, next to the antenna on the left (1 km from Los Abrigos), there is a

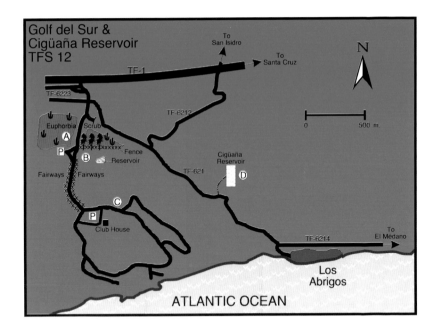

Golf del Sur &
Cigüaña Reservoir
TFS 12

lay-by just big enough for a few cars where you can park. Walk up the hill to view
the reservoir.

Strategy:
Walk around the low fence at the Golf Course to view the small reservoir and
surrounding areas. If you decide to go onto the course itself, do not forget to watch
out for golfers and be prepared to be questioned by the security guard.

Birds:
Year round: Little Egret, Grey Heron, Common Kestrel, Barbary Falcon, Moorhen,
Stone-curlew, Little Ringed Plover, Yellow-legged Gull, Rock Dove, Plain Swift,
Hoopoe, Berthelot´s Pipit, Grey Wagtail, Blackbird, Spectacled Warbler, Blackcap,
Canary Islands Chiffchaff, Southern Grey Shrike, Spanish Sparrow.
Summer visitors: Turtle Dove, Pallid Swift.
Winter visitors: Cattle Egret, Grey Plover, Whimbrel, Greenshank, Common
Sandpiper, Red-throated Pipit, White Wagtail, Starling.
Passage migrants: Spoonbill, Marsh Harrier, Spotted Crake*, Little Crake, Collared
Pratincole, Lapwing*, Little Stint*, Curlew Sandpiper*, Dunlin*, Ruff*, Common
Snipe*, Whimbrel*, Wood Sandpiper, Whiskered Tern, European Bee-eater, Short-
toed Lark, Skylark, Swallow*, Red-rumped Swallow, House Martin, Tawny Pipit,
Meadow Pipit, Blue-headed Wagtail*, Yellow Wagtail*, Common Redstart*,
Whinchat, Northern Wheatear*, Song Thrush*, Sedge Warbler, Subalpine Warbler,
Willow Warbler*, Spotted Flycatcher*, Woodchat Shrike*.
Accidentals: Merlin, Eleonora´s Falcon, American Golden Plover, Pectoral
Sandpiper, Buff-breasted Sandpiper, Gull-billed Tern, Crested Lark, Richard´s Pipit.
Escapes: Yellow-crowned Bishop, Monk Parakeet.
(Passage migrants and accidental birds with an asterisk * have been accepted by the
Spanish Rarities Committee,or have been recorded by the author).

● SOUTHERN AIRPORT AREA   TFS13
Category: none

Description:
This area used to be semi-desert scrub until it was cultivated. Its potential as a site is very under-estimated and it is under-watched, but birds are attracted to the reservoirs (A) and a few interesting migrant bird species have been recorded. The chicken farm (B) is probably the most reliable site in Tenerife to see wintering Cattle Egret.

As it is so close to the southern airport, this area is always worth a quick look during migration.

Time to visit:
The best time to look for migrants is during migration, September to November and February to June. The winter months are better if you are looking for Cattle Egret and other winter visitors.

Location:
From Santa Cruz: Take motorway TF-1 to Los Cristianos and exit at Aeropuerto del Sur (Salida 23). Be ready for a sharp right-hand turn onto a secondary road just

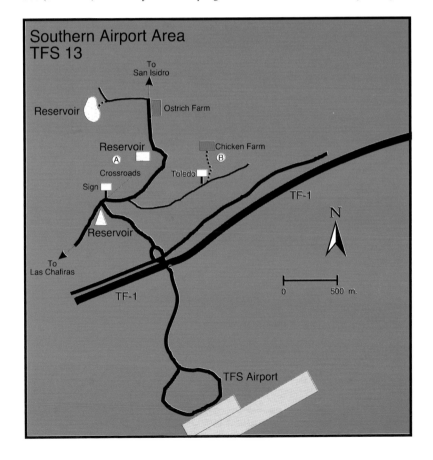

before the bridge. Head northwards up the road and turn left at the T-junction. You will see the first reservoir on your left. Park anywhere safe.

To visit the chicken farm (B), turn right at the crossroads (see sketch) and after about 0.9 km, turn left onto a dirt track at the sign to "Toledo". Stay on this track for 0.6 until you see the chicken farm. Beware of the strong smell!

To get to the second and third reservoirs (A) from the crossroads, follow the road up for 1km until you reach the second reservoir on your left. 0.8 km after this second reservoir turn left onto a dirt track that leads to the third reservoir. You will see the third reservoir on your left, after about 0.2 km. Be careful as this last reservoir is in a small gully!

From Las Americas/ Los Cristianos: Take motorway TF-1 to Santa Cruz and exit at Aeropuerto del Sur. Go left past the bridge and be ready for a sharp left turn onto a secondary road (Make sure you do not go straight on or head south). Follow this road up to the right and turn left at the T-junction. You will see the first reservoir on your left. Park anywhere safe.

To visit the chicken farm (B), turn right at the crossroads (see sketch) and after about 0.9 km, turn left onto a dirt track at the sign to "Toledo". Stay on this track for 0.6 until you see the chicken farm. Beware of the strong smell!

To get to the second and third reservoirs (A) from the crossroads, follow the road up for 1km until you reach the second on your left. 0.8 km after this second reservoir turn left onto a dirt track that leads to the third reservoir. You will see the third reservour on your left, after about 0.2 km. Be careful as this last reservoir is in a small gully!

Strategy:
Try not to be too exposed as birds might be flushed by your presence. At the first and third reservoirs, check the patchy vegetated corners.

Birds:
Year round: Little Egret, Grey Heron, Common Kestrel, Moorhen, Little Ringed Plover, Yellow-legged Gull, Rock Dove, Plain Swift, Berthelot´s Pipit, Grey Wagtail, Spectacled Warbler, Canary Islands Chiffchaff, Blue Tit, Spanish Sparrow, Linnet.
Summer visitors: Turtle Dove.
Winter visitors: Cattle Egret, Lapwing, Common Snipe, Greenshank, Green Sandpiper, Common Sandpiper, White Wagtail.
Passage migrants: Shoveler, Spotted Crake, Lapwing, Green Sandpiper, Swallow, House Martin.

Other wildlife:
Algerian Hedgehog.

● **EL MEDANO**   **TFS14**
Category: Special Natural Reserve

Description:
El Médano, whose name means "sand formations", is famous for La Mareta (C), a small salt-water lagoon, and the rocky coastal shores (A,B,D) on either sides of the main sandy beach. Montaña Roja, a volcanic cinder, dominates the landscape to the south.

La Mareta (C) is well located to attract migrant non-passerine bird species during passage. It has been watched over the past 25 years, and it is not unusual to find birds here that were originally reported at El Fraile Reservoir (TFS7).

The coastal rocky shores, (A,B,D), are the wintering grounds for a few waders and terns, and this is the only site on Tenerife where it is possible to see the last few breeding pairs of Kentish Plover. El Médano used to be an excellent place for Trumpeter Finch, Lesser Short-toed Lark and Stone-curlew, but now they are all scarce. The arrival of many Cory´s Shearwaters can be viewed from Punta del Bocinegro (D) in late February or early March, and Kittiwake can sometimes be seen in winter.

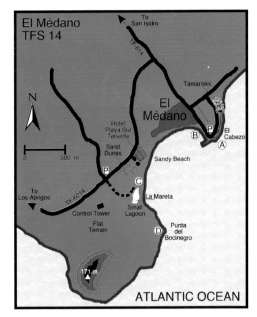

Time to visit:
Any time of the year should be good for resident bird species, but low tide in winter is the best time for waders. September to November, and February to June are best for migrants.

Location:
From Santa Cruz/ Las Americas/ Los Cristianos: Take motorway TF-1 to the El Médano exit (Salida 22). Follow the road towards the coast. To reach La Mareta (C) and Punta del Bocinegro (D), turn right at TF-6214, just by a fishing boat, to Los Abrigos. Park in the Nature Reserve car park and walk to the area.

Strategy:
Scan the shores of the lagoon to look for waders. A telescope will be very useful for the sites in El Médano. It is normally extremely windy here.

Birds:
Year round: Little Egret, Grey Heron, Common Kestrel, Stone-curlew, Little Ringed Plover, Kentish Plover, Yellow-legged Gull, Rock Dove, Collared Dove, Long-eared Owl, Plain Swift, Hoopoe, Lesser Short-toed Lark, Berthelot´s Pipit, Grey Wagtail, Spectacled Warbler, Canary Islands Chiffchaff, Southern Grey Shrike, Spanish Sparrow, Trumpeter Finch.
Summer visitors: Cory´s Shearwater, Common Tern, Turtle Dove, Pallid Swift.
Winter visitors: Ringed Plover, Kentish Plover, Grey Plover, Sanderling, Little Stint, Dunlin, Whimbrel, Curlew, Greenshank, Common Sandpiper, Turnstone, Audouin´s Gull, Black-headed Gull, Lesser Black-backed Gull, Sandwich Tern.
Passage migrants: Gannet, White Stork, Spoonbill, Black Kite, Marsh Harrier, Oystercatcher, Black-winged Stilt*, Avocet*, European Golden Plover, Lapwing, Knot, Little Stint, Temminck´s Stint, Curlew Sanpiper*, Dunlin*, Ruff, Black-tailed Godwit, Bar-tailed Godwit*, Spotted Redshank, Common Redshank*, Green Sanpiper, Great Skua*, Black-headed Gull, Little Tern, Common Swift, Swallow*,

House Martin*, Yellow Wagtail, White Wagtail*.
Accidentals: Glossy Ibis, Greylag Goose, Lanner Falcon, American Golden Plover, White-rumped Sandpiper, Pectoral Sandpiper, Lesser Yellowlegs, Ring-billed Gull*, Common Gull, Herring Gull, Great Black-backed Gull, Gull-billed Tern*, Woodpigeon, Calandra Lark.
(Passage migrants and accidental birds with an asterisk * have been accepted by the Spanish Rarities Committee, or have been recorded by the author).

Other wildlife:
Bottlenose Dolphin, Algerian Hedgehog, Rabbit, Canary Lizard.

Kentish Plover

TFS4 GUAZA MOUNTAIN

TFS7 EL FRAILE RESERVOIR

TFS11 AMARILLA GOLF COURSE

TFS14 EL MEDANO

THE SOUTHWEST (TFSW)

Barbary Partridge

THE SOUTHWEST (TFSW)

The Southwest is characterised by deep ravines and gorges, the most representative being Barranco del Infierno (TFSW1) or Hell´s Gorge. A small population of Barbary Partridge still survives in this protected area. Unfortunately, hunting is still a common practice on the island.

This is a very arid region, and the shortage of water limits agriculture. A few reservoirs (TFSW3 & TFSW4 & TFSW5) have been established to provide enough water for irrigating the banana and tomato plantations.

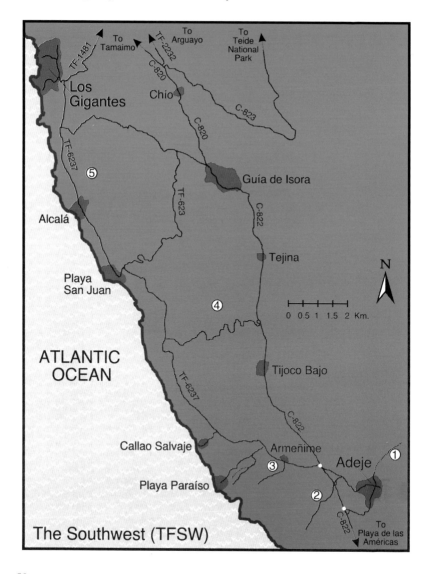

● BARRANCO DEL INFIERNO TFSW1
Category: Special Nature Reserve
(Hell´s Gorge)

Description:
This is one of the most popular and most visited "barrancos", and the only one on Tenerife with a natural waterfall. The trail is in very good condition and winds up through *euphorbia* vegetation to the end of the ravine-craggy vertical cliffs that make excellent nesting places for Cory´s Shearwater.
The number of resident birds is not very impressive, but Barranco del Infierno is probably the last stronghold of Barbary Partridge on Tenerife.

Time to visit:
Anytime during the year should produce the Partridge. It is adviseable to visit either early in the morning, or towards late afternoon.

Location:
From Santa Cruz/ Las Americas/ Los Cristianos: Take motorway TF-1 to C-822. Exit on Adeje (TF-5121) and drive up towards the town. At the roundabout, turn right onto a main street and left at the signpost to "Barranco del Infierno". Follow this sign and park near a bar/restaurant called Otero, where the trail starts.

Strategy:
Walk up the trail. A good place to see Sardinian Warbler is at the corner by the old water-bridge, just after the first three viewpoints and before the viewpoint with the signpost to "Acequia Larga". Barbary Partridges occur more frequently on the slopes, about 100 metres on from this last viewpoint, and can be located by their typical "ka-ke-lick" sound. To be sure of hearing this call, an early morning or late afternoon visit is crucial.

Birds:
Year round: Sparrowhawk, Common Buzzard, Common Kestrel, Barbary Partridge, Yellow-legged Gull, Rock Dove, Barn Owl, Long-eared Owl, Plain Swift, Hoopoe, Berthelot´s Pipit, Grey Wagtail, Robin, Blackbird, Spectacled Warbler, Sardinian Warbler, Blackcap, Canary Islands Chiffchaff, Blue Tit, Raven, Spanish Sparrow, Canary, Linnet.
Summer visitors: Cory´s Shearwater, Turtle Dove.

Other wildlife:
Butterflies: African Migrant, Bath White, Canary Blue, Canary Speckled Wood, Clouded Yellow, Indian Red Admiral, Monarch, Painted Lady, Plain Tiger, Red Admiral, Small Copper, Small White.

Barbary Partridge

● COSTA ADEJE GOLF COURSE   TFSW2
Category: none

Description:
This golf course was opened in 1998. Like the other golf courses on Tenerife, it could become an interesting site in the next few years.

Time to visit:
The best times are during autumn and spring migration.

Location:
From Santa Cruz/ Las Americas/ Los Cristianos: Take motorway TF-1 to C-822. Make a U-turn at the roundabout and turn right to "Golf Costa Adeje".

Strategy:
Scan the fairways with a telescope and try checking the trees and bushes for migrants. Remember that golfers have priority at all times.

Birds:
Year round: Common Kestrel, Little Ringed Plover, Yellow-legged Gull, Rock Dove, Plain Swift, Hoopoe Berthelot´s Pipit, Grey Wagtail, Spanish Sparrow.
Summer visitors: Turtle Dove, Pallid Swift.
Winter visitors: Whimbrel, Lesser Black-backed Gull, White Wagtail.

● ARMEÑIME RESERVOIRS   TFSW3
Category: none

Description:
These four reservoirs have been under-watched but have proven to be as important as the others in the south of Tenerife. Presa Vieja (A) is located near the town of Armeñime. It is very dirty and untidy, but does attract a few migrants during passage. Presa de Curbelo (B) is a much larger reservoir and is famous for attracting North American Ducks. The Playa Paraiso Reservoirs (C) are rather small, but they hold the biggest population of Moorhen in Tenerife and have attracted a few interesting migrants in the past.

Time to visit:
The best times to visit are during autumn and spring migration and in winter (September-June).

Location:
From Santa Cruz/ Las Americas/ Los Cristianos: Take motorway TF-1 to C-822 and turn left at the roundabout to Playa San Juan (TF-6237).
To reach Presa Vieja (A), turn right at Armeñime and take the first right, which is a dead-end. Park anywhere safe.
To get to Presa de Curbelo (B) from the roundabout, turn left after 1 km to "El Puertito". Follow this road for 1.4 km and park at the lay-by on your right, near a an abondened field with concrete walls with holes. Walk northwards to reach the reservoir.
For Playa Paraiso Reservoirs (C), turn left to Playa Paraiso. After 0.2 km, turn left at the sign to "El Pinque". You will see the reservoir on your right after about 0.7 km. Continue on the track to reach the other reservoir.

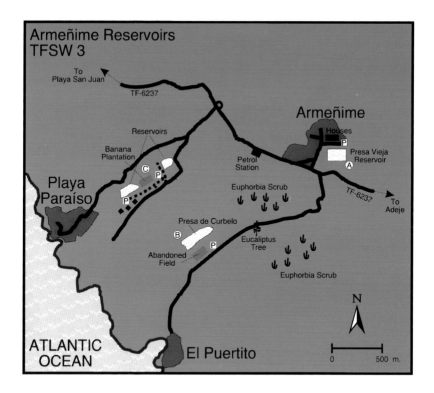

Strategy:
To check the reservoirs it is recommended that you be as silent as possible as birds might be flushed by your presence. For Presa de Curbelo (B) a telescope is essential. Check the vegetated area on the Playa Paraiso Reservoirs.

Birds:
Year round: Little Egret, Grey Heron, Common Kestrel, Moorhen, Coot, Little Ringed Plover, Yellow-legged Gull, Rock Dove, Plain Swift, Hoopoe, Berthelot's Pipit, Grey Wagtail, Blackbird, Spectacled Warbler, Blackcap, Canary Islands Chiffchaff, Blue Tit, Spanish Sparrow, Goldfinch.
Summer visitors: Turtle Dove, Pallid Swift.
Winter visitors: Coot, Grey Plover, Greenshank, Common Sandpiper, Lesser Black-backed Gull, White Wagtail.
Passage migrants: Little Bittern*, Night Heron*, Squacco Heron*, Purple Heron*, Garganey*, Black-winged Stilt, Lapwing*, Curlew Sandpiper*, Dunlin*, Ruff*, Common Snipe*, Black-tailed Godwit*, Wood Sandpiper*, Swallow*, House Martin*.
Accidentals: Ring-necked Duck*.
(Passage migrants and accidental birds with an asterisk * have been accepted by the Spanish Rarities Committee, or have been recorded by the author).

● LAGO ABAMA   TFSW4
Category: none

Description:
This is a fairly large reservoir although not as big as a lake, as the Spanish name implies. Water levels are normally low, but it holds a few breeding pairs of Moorhen and Coot. The non-native bushes on the slopes have attracted passerine migrants in the past, and transatlantic vagrants have been recorded here although, in general, the reservoir is under-watched for its potential.
Osprey is sometimes seen fishing in the area.

Time to visit:
The best time to visit is during autumn (September to November) and spring migration (February to June), but a winter visit could also be rewarding.

Location:
From Santa Cruz/ Las Americas/ Los Cristianos: Take motorway TF-1 to C-822 and head for Guía de Isora. You pass through the town of Menores and turn off towards Vera de Erques/Playa San Juan (TF-6233). Follow the signs to Playa San Juan and after about 1.7 km, park near the garden. Ignore the chains and walk to the reservoir as indicated on the sketch.

Strategy:
Walk along the road until you get to a dirt track that will lead you to the main reservoir. The best approach for this reservoir is to walk all the way to the south-west corner and then use a telescope to look for birds. Try to make as little noise as possible as the birds here are very frightened by the presence of humans.

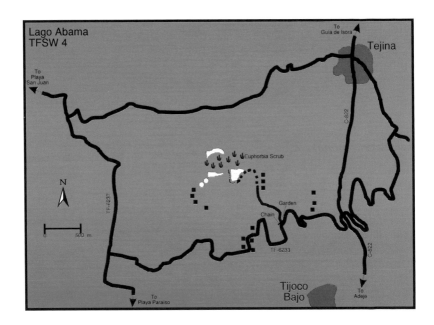

Birds:
Year round: Little Egret, Grey Heron, Osprey, Common Kestrel, Moorhen, Coot, Stone-curlew, Little Ringed Plover, Yellow-legged Gull, Rock Dove, Plain Swift, Hoopoe, Berthelot´s Pipit, Grey Wagtail, Spectacled Warbler, Sardinian Warbler, Blackcap, Canary Islands Chiffchaff, Blue Tit, Spanish Sparrow, Goldfinch, Linnet.
Summer visitors: Turtle Dove, Pallid Swift.
Winter visitors: Coot, Common Snipe, Curlew, Greenshank, Common Sandpiper, White Wagtail.
Passage migrants: Common Teal*, Osprey*, Lapwing*, Curlew Sandpiper*, Ruff*, Swallow*, House Martin*, Yellow Wagtail*, Black Redstart*, Northern Wheatear*, Chiffchaff sp*.
Accidentals: American Golden Plover*.
(Passage migrants and accidental birds with an asterisk * have been accepted by the Spanish Rarities Committee, or have been recorded by the author).

● PUNTA BLANCA RESERVOIR   TFSW5
Category: none

Description:
This small reservoir is located in a little gully and has a very poor list, but it is worth a quick visit, especially if you are staying close by in Los Gigantes. Perhaps the most interesting bird recorded in the area is Woodcock, which can sometimes be seen at dusk on the access roads to the reservoir.

Time to visit:
The best times are during autumn and spring migration.

Location:
From Santa Cruz/ Las Americas/ Los Cristianos: Take motorway TF-1 to C-822 and turn left at the roundabout to Playa San Juan (TF-6237). After passing through Playa San Juan and Alcalá, look for the petrol station on your left. 0.8 km after the petrol station, turn right onto a secondary road sign-posted to Cooragricola (painted on the wall). 0.4 km along the road, there is a small reservoir that is worth a quick look, just in case. Follow the road up for 0.5 km and then turn left. When you see a blue door, turn right. If it is open,

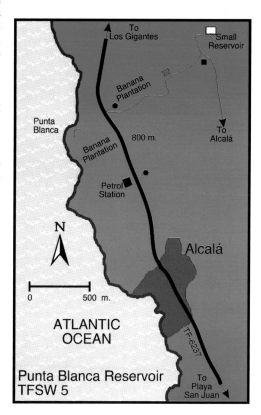

Punta Blanca Reservoir
TFSW 5

go through the blue door, if not, ask permission to get in. You will see the reservoir on your left.

From Los Gigantes: Take TF-6237 to Alcala. 0.8 km from the petrol station near Alcala, turn left onto a secondary road sign-posted Cooragricola (painted on the wall). 0.4 km from here, there is a small reservoir that is worth a quick look, just in case. Follow the road up for 0.5 km and then turn left. Carry on and turn right when you come to a blue door. If it is open, go through the door, if not, ask permission to go in. You will see the reservoir on your left.

Strategy:
It is best to wait until dusk to look for Woodcock as they get frightened from the roadside by traffic.

Birds:
Year round: Little Egret, Grey Heron, Common Kestrel, Moorhen, Woodcock, Yellow-legged Gull, Rock Dove, Plain Swift, Berthelot´s Pipit, Grey Wagtail, Blackbird, Sardinian Warbler, Blackcap, Canary Islands Chiffchaff, Blue Tit, Spanish Sparrow.
Summer visitors: Turtle Dove.
Winter visitors: Coot, Common Sandpiper.
Passage migrants: Swallow, House Martin.

Spectacled Warbler

TFSW1 BARRANCO DEL INFIERNO (HELL'S GORGE)

TFSW2 COSTA ADEJE

TFSW3 ARMEÑIME RESERVOIRS (PLAYA PARAISO RESERVOIR)

TFSW4 LAGO ABAMA

THE NORTHWEST (TFNW)

Barbary Falcon

THE NORTHWEST
(TFNW)

ATLANTIC OCE

This ancient massif is characterised by steep coastal cliffs and gullies (TFNW6), which are the year-round home for a few pairs of Ospreys and Barbary Falcons. The northern slopes of the cliffs are covered by a dense laurel forest, which holds healthy populations of both of Tenerife´s endemic pigeons (TFNW3). This region belongs to Teno Rural Park, and its human residents still retain a rural way of life in close contact with nature. It is probably for this reason that a few bird species have their last stronghold here. Rock Sparrow and the last surviving pairs of Ravens can easily be found in the Northwest of Tenerife (TFNW1, TFNW2, TFNW4, TFNW5, TFNW6).

● ARGUAYO   TFNW1
Category: none

Description:
This is a small town on the way to Santiago del Teide, where Rock Sparrow has been recorded sitting on the electric wires.

Time to visit:
All year round.

Location:
From Las Americas/ Los Cristianos: Take motorway TF-1 to C-822, and head towards Guía de Isora. Go as far as the village of Chío and then turn right to Arguayo.

From Puerto de la Cruz: Take motorway TF-5 (Autopista del Norte) to C-820 Icod de los Vinos. Exit at TF-222 La Guancha/ Icod de los Vinos. Follow the signs for Icod de los Vinos and turn right at the T-junction. Pass through Icod de los Vinos, and at the roundabout turn left to C-820 marked El Tanque/ Guía de Isora. Carry on until you reach Santiago del Teide, then turn left to Arguayo.

Strategy:
Check the wires for Rock Sparrow.

Birds:
Year round: Common Kestrel, Rock Dove, Plain Swift, Berthelot´s Pipit, Blue Tit, Rock Sparrow, Canary.

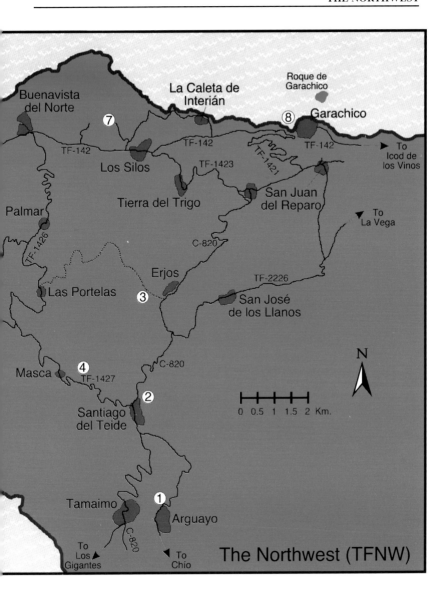

The Northwest (TFNW)

● SANTIAGO DEL TEIDE   TFNW2
Category: none

Description:

This town is located on the limits of Teno Rural Park. The fields and wires to the south of the town are good for Rock Sparrow and Corn Bunting.

Time to visit:

All year round.

Location:
From Las Americas/ Los Cristianos: Take motorway TF-1 to C-822, and head for
Guía de Isora. Keep on C-820, passing through Tamaimo, until you reach Santiago
del Teide.

From Puerto de la Cruz: Take motorway TF-5 (Autopista del Norte) to C-820, signposted Icod de los Vinos. Exit on TF-222 La Guancha/ Icod de los Vinos. Follow
the signs and turn right at the T-junction to Icod de los Vinos. Pass through Icod de
los Vinos and turn left at the roundabout onto C-820 to El Tanque/ Guía de Isora.
Keep on this road until you get to Santiago del Teide.

Strategy:
Check the electric wires for Rock Sparrow and Corn Bunting. Canaries are common
at the small picnic site with eucaliptus trees.

Birds:
Year round: Common Kestrel, Rock Dove, Plain Swift, Berthelot´s Pipit, Blue Tit,
Rock Sparrow, Canary, Corn Bunting.

● MONTE DEL AGUA & ERJOS PONDS TFNW3
Category: Teno Rural Park

Description:
This is a forested mountainous region at the head of the Barranco de los Cochinos
and is the only place in Tenerife where Manx Shearwater is known to breed.
Monte del Agua is one of the last remaining undisturbed areas of laurel forest on
the island, and the two endemic pigeons can be found here. This unique forest is
characterised by steep slopes, densely covered with laurel-like trees of different
sizes, some with lichen on their trunks. It is also possible to see ferns and several
other interesting endemic plants and butterflies in this area. The forest is often
covered with mist, which makes visibility a serious problem.
Pigeon watching requires a great deal of patience, and they are most frequently
seen flying very fast over the canopy. Only occasionally can they be seen perched,
and this is usually during the breeding season.

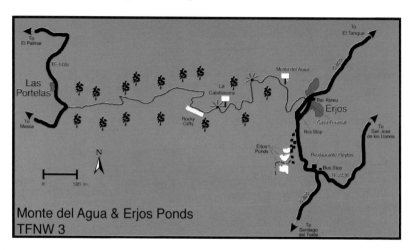

Previous soil extraction and the impermeability of this region have created a series of artificial ponds, which have been colonised by aquatic plants. There is a stable population of breeding Moorhens at Erjos Ponds, and a few interesting passerine bird species can be observed around the ponds.

Time to visit:
The best time to look for pigeons is before and during the breeding season when males are flight-displaying over the canopy and showing their distinctive tails. Bolle´s Pigeon breeds from January to September, and Laurel Pigeon breeds mainly from May to September although sometimes earlier. Unless you are extremely patient, it is adviseable not to visit between October and December.
An early morning or late afternoon visit is crucial, as the pigeons are more active at these times. Bear in mind the fact that it is often very misty.
The best time to visit the ponds to look for migrants is during the migratory periods.

Location:
From Puerto de la Cruz: Take motorway TF-5 (Autopista del Norte) to C-820, and head for Icod de los Vinos. Exit onto TF-222 to La Guancha/ Icod de los Vinos. Follow the signs and turn right at the T-junction to Icod de los Vinos. Go through Icod de los Vinos and turn left at the roundabout onto C-820 to El Tanque/ Guía de Isora. The village of Erjos is about 9.5 km from El Tanque. Once in Erjos, turn right onto a rough track and after about 0.5 km, you will get to Monte del Agua. The "Casa Forestal" is just near the track entrance. (Go past the Abreu bar on your left and look for a big pine tree to the right).
The turn-off to Erjos Ponds is 0.2 km from the turning to Monte del Agua.

From Las Americas/ Los Cristianos: Take motorway TF-1 to C-822, and head for Guía de Isora. Continue along C-820 to Santiago del Teide and Erjos. The turning for Erjos Ponds is 1 km from the San José de los Llanos junction (TF-2226) ("Restaurante Fleytas"). After about 0.2 km, you will see a rough track near the "Casa Forestal" that leads to Monte del Agua. (Look for a big pine tree on your left).

Strategy:
A 4WD vehicle is recommended for visiting Monte del Agua. One of the most popular vantagepoints is about 5km from the start of the rough track. Park near the sign to La Calabacera, close to the rock with a rain gauge on top of it, and then take the trail down to the vantagepoint. This trail can be very slippery, so be careful.
The Rocky Cliff to the west, is much better for observing both species of pigeon. Park in the lay-by, which is only big enough for one vehicle. Look up to the wall and you should see pigeons flying around at high speeds. To see the pigeons in flight, scour the entire area from a vantagepoint and always follow the pigeon with binoculars until it is not longer in sight. This is the only way to locate a bird that decides to perch on an exposed branch or rock.

Birds:
Year round: Grey Heron, Sparrowhawk, Common Buzzard, Common Kestrel, Barbary Partridge, Moorhen, Woodcock, Yellow-legged Gull, Rock Dove, Bolle´s Pigeon, Laurel Pigeon, Barn Owl, Long-eared Owl, Plain Swift, Berthelot´s Pipit, Grey Wagtail, Robin, Blackbird, Spectacled Warbler, Sardinian Warbler, Blackcap, Canary Islands Chiffchaff, Canary Islands Kinglet, Blue Tit, Raven, Spanish Sparrow, Chaffinch, Canary, Greenfinch, Linnet, Corn Bunting.
Summer visitors: Manx Shearwater, Turtle Dove, Pallid Swift.

Winter visitors: Coot, Common Snipe, Common Sandpiper.
Passage migrants: Short-toed Eagle, Booted Eagle, Common Snipe, Alpine Swift, Melodious Warbler, Willow Warbler.
Accidentals: Ring-necked Duck, Eleonora´s Falcon, Woodpigeon.

Other wildlife:
Reptiles: Canary Lizard.
Butterflies: American Painted Lady, Bath White, Canary Blue, Canary Speckled Wood, Cardinal, Canarian Cleopatra, Clouded Yellow, Indian Red Admiral, Lulworth Skipper, Meadow Brown, Painted Lady, Queen of Spain Fritillary, Red Admiral, Small Copper, Small White.

● ROAD TO MASCA   TFNW4
Category: Teno Rural Park

Description:
This is a very narrow road carved out of the spectacular Los Gigantes cliffs. It is a popular tourist destination and worth visiting if you have enough time.

Time to visit:
You should be able to see a few resident species all year round.

Location:
From Santa Cruz/ Puerto de La Cruz: Take motorway TF-5 (Autopista del Norte) to Icod de los Vinos (C-820). From here follow TF-142 to Buenavista, passing through Garachico and Los Silos. At Buenavista turn left to El Palmar (TF-1426) and Masca.

From Las Americas/ Los Cristianos: Take motorway TF-1 to the C-822 to Guía de Isora. Keep on C-820, passing through Tamaimo until you get to Santiago del Teide. At Santiago del Teide turn left onto TF-1427 to Masca.

Strategy:
This is an extremely windy road, so be very careful. Follow the road and stop at the viewpoints to look for raptors and passerine bird species.

Birds:
Year round: Common Buzzard, Common Kestrel, Barbary Partridge, Yellow-legged Gull, Rock Dove, Plain Swift, Berthelot´s Pipit, Grey Wagtail, Blackbird, Spectacled Warbler, Sardinian Warbler, Blackcap, Canary Islands Chiffchaff, Blue Tit, Raven, Spanish Sparrow, Canary.
Summer visitors: Turtle Dove.

● TENO ALTO   TFNW5
Category: Teno Rural Park

Description:
This is an area of cultivated lots (terraces) and stoney plains, and is famous for its goat cheese. The small town of Teno Alto is quite enchanting and takes you back in time. From an ornithological point of view, it is an interesting spot as it is the only reliable breeding site for Rock Sparrow.

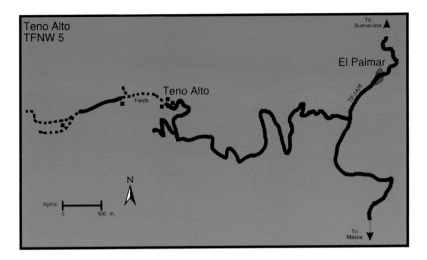

Time to visit:
It is possible to visit all year round, but try to avoid the winter months (December to February) when Rock Sparrow moves down to the lower zone of Teno Natural Park (TFNW6).

Location:
From Santa Cruz/ Puerto de La Cruz: Take motorway TF-5 (Autopista del Norte) to Icod de los Vinos (C-820). From Icod de los Vinos follow TF-142 to Buenavista, passing through Garachico and Los Silos. At Buenavista turn left to El Palmar (TF-1426) and Masca. Turn right to Teno Alto.

From Las Americas/ Los Cristianos: Take motorway TF-1 to C-822 to Guía de Isora. Stay on C-820 to Santiago del Teide, passing through Tamaimo. At Santiago del Teide turn left onto TF-1427 to Masca. Near the village of El Palmar, turn left to Teno Alto.

Strategy:
Check the wires and fences near the stoney walls for Rock Sparrow as this is their breeding ground. If you cannot see them immediately, wait a few minutes or try locating them from their typical "pey-i" call.

Rock Sparrow

Birds:

<u>Year round:</u> Sparrowhawk, Common Buzzard, Common Kestrel, Barbary Falcon, Barbary Partridge, Yellow-legged Gull, Rock Dove, Plain Swift, Berthelot's Pipit, Grey Wagtail, Robin, Blackbird, Spectacled Warbler, Sardinian Warbler, Blackcap, Canary Islands Chiffchaff, Canary Islands Kinglet, Blue Tit, Raven, Spanish Sparrow, Rock Sparrow, Chaffinch, Canary, Linnet, Corn Bunting.
<u>Summer visitors:</u> Turtle Dove, Pallid Swift.

● TENO NATURAL PARK   TFNW6
Category: Teno Rural Park

Description:

This Natural Park at the western end of the Island is characterised by massive coastal cliffs which drop down into the sea (A & D), and by a flat coastal area, known locally as "Isla Baja" (B), which is dominated by *euphorbia* plants. The sea cliffs at Punta del Fraile (A) are considered to be the most reliable and easily accessible site in Tenerife for Barbary Falcon. Although the few pairs of Osprey tend to breed on the inaccesible cliffs to the southwest of the park (D), they can occasionally be seen from Punta del Fraile (A). Tomatoes are grown in the fields near the coast (B), and a few migrants have been recorded here.

There is a small sandy beach near the lighthouse, which is a good vantagepoint for seawatching (C). It is a particularly good spot for Cory's, Manx and Little Shearwater. A few interesting seabirds have been recorded at this site, and it actually has one of the highest seawatching counts in Tenerife.

The access road to the park is in good condition, but the area can be dangerous, as it is prone to strong winds and falling rocks.

Time to visit:

You should be able to see Barbary Falcon all year round, but midday in the spring and summer when it is nice and hot, is the best time of all.

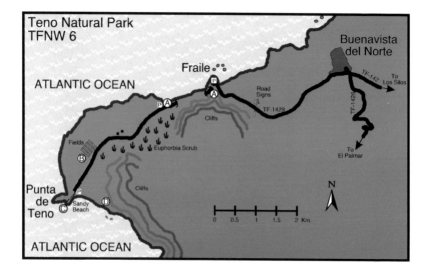

Barbary Falcon

Migrants occur between September and November, and February and June. If you are looking for big flocks of Rock Sparrows, December to February is the best time. March to September is best for seawatching.

Location:
From Santa Cruz/ Puerto de La Cruz: Take motorway TF-5 (Autopista del Norte) to C-820 to Icod de los Vinos. From Icod de los Vinos, follow TF-142 to Buenavista, passing through Garachico and Los Silos. At Buenavista take TF-1429 and follow the signs for "Parque Natural Punta de Teno". After 4.2 km, you will reach the viewpoint where you can leave your car. Beware of strong winds!

From Las Americas/ Los Cristianos: Take motorway TF-1 to C-822 to Guía de Isora. Follow C-820, passing through Santiago del Teide and Erjos. 9.5 km after Erjos, turn left onto TF-1421 to Garachico, which you come to about 8.5 km along the road. Turn left onto TF-142 to Buenavista, passing through Los Silos, then at Buenavista take TF-1429, and follow the sign to "Parque Natural Punta de Teno". Park at the first viewpoint. Beware of strong winds!

Strategy:
Barbary Falcon frequents the cliffs above Punta del Fraile (A), and they can either be seen perched on the rocky crags, or patrolling the skies above. If you are lucky, you will be able to see them hunting for Rock Dove. Walk around the fields (B), which are sometimes cultivated with tomatoes to look for wintering Rock Sparrow and larks. A telescope is essential for seawatching from Punta de Teno (C).

Birds:
Year round: Little Shearwater, Little Egret, Common Buzzard, Osprey, Common Kestrel, Barbary Falcon, Barbary Partridge, Yellow-legged Gull, Rock Dove, Plain Swift, Berthelot´s Pipit, Spectacled Warbler, Sardinian Warbler, Canary Islands Chiffchaff, Blue Tit, Raven, Spanish Sparrow, Rock Sparrow, Canary, Linnet, Corn Bunting.
Summer visitors: Bulwer´s Petrel, Cory´s Shearwater, Manx Shearwater, European Storm-petrel, Turtle Dove, Pallid Swift.
Winter visitors: Skylark.
Passage migrants: White Stork, Montagu´s Harrier, Peregrine Falcon, Great Skua, Pomarine Skua, Short-toed Lark.
Accidentals: Red-billed Tropicbird, Mistle Thrush.

● LOS SILOS AREA   TFNW7
Category: Scientific Interest

Description:
This area is made up of banana plantations and a few scattered reservoirs. Taco Mountain Reservoir (A) and Los Silos Reservoirs (B) have attracted some very interesting migrants, and the area near the lighthouse (C) is good for seawatching. The rocky shore of Caleta de Interian, known as "El Bajío" (D), provides an intertidal zone exposed at low tide which is good for waders and terns in winter.

Time to visit:
The best times to visit are during migration - September to November, and February to June. Low tide during the winter months is the best time for waders.

Location:
From Santa Curz/ Puerto de La Cruz: Take motorway TF-5 (Autopista del Norte) to Icod de los Vinos (C-820). Stay on TF-142, passing through Garachico, until you get to Buenavista.
If you are going to Taco Mountain Reservoir (A), go through Los Silos and turn right after 1.9 km to "Balsa de la Montaña de Taco". Be careful because it is not signposted. Follow the road to the gate. Park and walk to the reservoir.
To get to Los Silos Reservoirs (B), turn right at the petrol station just after Los Silos, and take the second left to "Cementerio". The first reservoir is on your right. If you follow this road for 0.7 km, passing a cemetery on the left, you will come to the second reservoir, which is on the right. Park near the yellow gate.
To get to El Bajío (D), turn right to "La Caleta de Interian" (2 km from the Garachico viewpoint). At the T-junction, turn right and park near the sandy beach.
To get approach the lighthouse (C), turn right at the petrol station just after Los Silos, and follow the road to the dirt track at "El Puertito".

From Las Americas/ Los Cristianos: Take motorway TF-1 to the C-822 to Guía de Isora. Stay on C-820, passing through Santiago del Teide and Erjos, then about 9.5 km after Erjos, turn left onto TF-1421 to Garachico. After 8.5 km, you will come to Garachico where you turn left onto TF-142 (in the direction of Buenavista) to get to Los Silos.
To reach Taco Mountain Reservoir (A), go through Los Silos and turn right after 1.9 km to "Balsa de la Montaña de Taco". Be careful because it is not signposted. Follow the road to the gate. Park and walk to the reservoir.
To get to Los Silos Reservoirs (B), turn right at the petrol station just after Los Silos, and take the second left to "Cementerio". The first reservoir is on your right. Stay on this road for 0.7 km, passing a cemetery on your left, and you will get to the second reservoir, which will be on your right. Park near the yellow gate.
To get to El Bajío (D) turn right to "La Caleta de Interian" (2 km from the Garachico viewpoint). At the T-junction, turn right and park near the sandy beach.
To approach the lighthouse (C), turn right at the petrol station just after Los Silos, and follow the road to the dirt track at "El Puertito".

Strategy:
Try not to be too exposed when checking the reservoirs as the birds might be flushed by your presence.

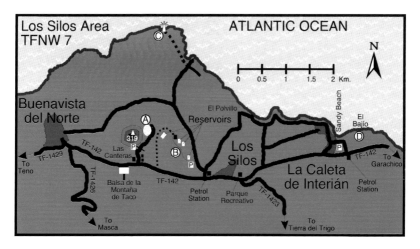

Birds:

Year round: Little Egret, Grey Heron, Common Buzzard, Osprey, Common Kestrel, Barbary Falcon, Moorhen, Coot, Yellow-legged Gull, Rock Dove, Collared Dove, Long-eared Owl, Plain Swift, Berthelot´s Pipit, Grey Wagtail, Blackbird, Spectacled Warbler, Sardinian Warbler, Blackcap, Canary Islands Chiffchaff, Blue Tit, Spanish Sparrow, Canary, Goldfinch, Linnet.

Summer visitors: Cory´s Shearwater, Turtle Dove, Pallid Swift.

Winter visitors: Wigeon, Common Teal, Grey Plover, Common Snipe, Whimbrel, Greenshank, Green Sandpiper, Wood Sandpiper, Common Sandpiper, Turnstone, Lesser Black-backed Gull, Sandwich Tern, White Wagtail.

Passage migrants: Night Heron*, Squacco Heron*, Oystercatcher*, Cream-coloured Courser*, Wood Sandpiper*, Short-eared Owl*, Sand Martin*, Swallow*, House Martin*, Meadow Pipit*, Yellow Wagtail*, Black Redstart*, Northern Wheatear*.

Accidentals: Pied-billed Grebe*, Ring-necked Duck*, Scaup, Lesser Yellowlegs*. (Passage migrants and accidental birds with an asterisk * have been accepted by the Spanish Rarities Committee, or have been recorded by the author).

● ROQUE DE GARACHICO   TFNW8
Category: Natural Monument

Description:

This small islet off Garachico is of ornithological importance as it is the breeding ground for Little Shearwater. There is also a large Yellow-legged Gull colony on the rock, and it is not uncommon to see Little Egret and Grey Heron here too.

Time to visit:

You can visit all year round. The best time of day to look for shearwaters is late afternoon when they get closer to land.

Location:

From Santa Cruz/ Puerto de La Cruz: Take motorway TF-5 (Autopista del Norte) to Icod de los Vinos (C-820). Stay on TF-142 to Buenavista, passing through Garachico. Park in the car park on your right, about 0.5 km from Garachico. (Look for a statue on your right).

From Las Americas/ Los Cristianos: Take motorway TF-1 to C-822 to Guía de Isora. Stay on C-820, passing through Santiago del Teide and Erjos. 9.5 km after Erjos, turn left onto TF-1421 to Garachico, which is about 8.5 km along the road. Then, turn left onto TF-142 (Buenavista) to get to Los Silos. Park in the car park by the statue on the right.

Strategy:
A telescope is essential to look for shearwaters. Try to visit this site late in the afternoon, as this is when they come ashore.

Birds:
Year round: Little Shearwater, Little Egret, Grey Heron, Yellow-legged Gull.
Summer visitors: Cory´s Shearwater.

Cory's Shearwater

TFNW3 ERJOS PONDS

TFNW4 MASCA

TFNW6 TENO NATURAL PARK
(PUNTA DEL FRAILE)

TFNW6 TENO NATURAL PARK

THE NORTH (TFN)

Laurel Pigeon

THE NORTH (TFN)

The North of Tenerife has been severely affected by urban development, tourist resorts and cultivation. However, it is here where both endemic pigeons are more accessible (TFN3), and where Blue Chaffinch can reliably be found, together with the smaller endemic race of Chaffinch (TFN2). The Cruz Santa Reservoir (TFN4) is the biggest body of water on Tenerife and has attracted a few interesting migrants.

● **PLAYA DEL CASTILLO**
& LORO PARK   **TFN1**
Category: none

Description:
This is a small sandy beach, which is home to a population of Yellow-legged Gull, and in the past, the occasional Ring-billed Gull has been recorded. If you are in the area, it is worth a quick visit.
Loro Park is a zoological park with thousands of parrots in captivity. Two of the commoner species that breed in the wild are Ring-necked Parakeet and Monk Parakeet.

Time to visit:
The best time to visit is during migration or in winter (September to June).

Location:
From Santa Cruz: Take motorway TF-5 (Autopista del Norte) to the Puerto de la Cruz exit. Follow the signs to Loro Park, and you will see the sandy beach on your right, just before the entrance to the park.

From Las Americas/ Los Cristianos: Take TF-1 to Santa Cruz and exit on Parque Nacional del Teide. Follow the signs for Vilaflor and Parque Nacional del Teide. Cross the National Park on the C-821, and head towards la Orotava and Puerto de la Cruz. Once in Puerto de la Cruz, follow the signs to Loro Park and you will see the sandy beach on your right, just before the entrance to the park.

Strategy:
Check the gulls and other birds, preferably with a telescope.

Birds:
Year round: Common Kestrel, Yellow-legged Gull, Rock Dove, Collared Dove, Ring-necked Parakeet, Monk Parakeet, Plain Swift, Grey Wagtail, Blackbird, Canary Islands Chiffchaff, Blue Tit, Spanish Sparrow, Canary.
Summer visitors: Cory´s Shearwater.

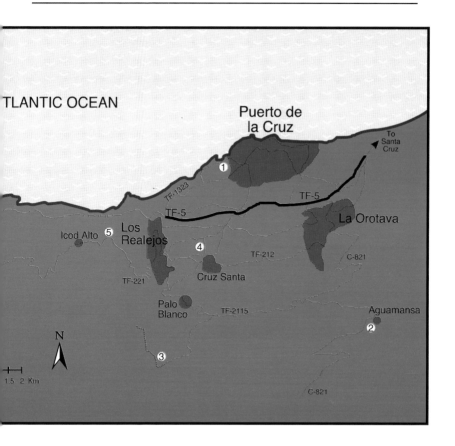

Winter visitors: Whimbrel, Common Sandpiper, Turnstone, Lesser Black-backed Gull, Sandwich Tern.
Accidentals: Ring-billed Gull*.
(Accidental birds with an asterisk * have been accepted by the Spanish Rarities Committee, or have been recorded by the author).

Other wildlife:
Canary Lizard, Canary Skink.

● LA CALDERA   TFN2
Category: Natural Park

Description:
This picnic site is one of the few areas on Tenerife where there is a mixture of habitats, and it provides the right conditions for Blue and Common Chaffinch to coexist. The vegetation is mainly pine forest, but there is fayal-brezal too. This site is normally shrouded in thick cloud or mist.

Time to visit:
All seasons except winter when it is prone to being cold and misty.

Location:
From Santa Cruz: Take motorway TF-5 (Autopista del Norte) to La Orotava/ Las Cañadas del Teide C-821 (Salida 17) exit. At the roundabout in La Orotava turn left and go up the hill. Follow the signs for Parque Nacional del Teide and turn left onto C-821. About 12.7 km past La Orotava, and after the 16 KM sign, turn left to "Zona Recreativa la Caldera". The picnic area and car park are about 1 km.

From Puerto de la Cruz: Take motorway TF-5 (Autopista del Norte) to Santa Cruz and exit at La Orotava/ Las Cañadas del Teide C-821 (Salida 17). At the roundabout in La Orotava, turn left and go up the hill. Follow the signs for Parque Nacional del Teide and turn left onto C-821. About 12.7 km past La Orotava, and after the 16 KM sign, turn left to "Zona Recreativa la Caldera". The picnic area and car park are about 1 km.

From Las Americas/ Los Cristianos: Take TF-1 to Santa Cruz and exit at Parque Nacional del Teide. Follow the signs for Vilaflor and Parque Nacional del Teide. Cross the National Park on the C-821 to La Orotava. Before you get to Aguamasa, turn right to "Zona Recreativa la Caldera". The picnic area and car park are about 1 km.

Strategy:
Walk around near the bar/restaurant to look for Blue and Common Chaffinch. Canary Islands Kinglet occurs in the tree heaths around the picnic tables. In addition, check the fountains for birds.

Birds:
Year round: Sparrowhawk, Common Buzzard, Common Kestrel, Rock Dove, Bolle´s Pigeon, Laurel Pigeon, Plain Swift, Berthelot´s Pipit, Grey Wagtail, Robin, Blackbird, Blackcap, Canary Islands Chiffchaff, Canary Islands Kinglet, Blue Tit, Chaffinch, Blue Chaffinch, Canary, Greenfinch.
Summer visitors: Turtle Dove, Pallid Swift.

● **LADERA DE TIGAIGA**   **TFN3**
Category: Natural Park
(Chanajiga or Chanajija)

Description:
This is a small patch of laurel forest where the two endemic pigeons can be found. To reach the site, you have to pass through some agriculture fields that are good for Berthelot´s Pipit and Canary. At the start of the forest track there is a picnic area called "Zona Recreativa Chanajija", which is a good place for Chaffinch, Blue Tit and Robin. The track is in good condition although there is often a lot of mist or cloud. However, if you are looking for both endemic pigeons, this is the place to visit as it is the most accessible and reliable.

Time to visit:
The best time to look for pigeons is during the breeding season when males will be flight-displaying over the canopy and showing their distinctive tails. Bolle´s Pigeon breeds from January to September, and Laurel Pigeon mainly from May to September although sometimes earlier. Unless you are very patient, it is not a good idea to visit from October to December.
It is adviseable to visit early morning or late afternoon as this is when the pigeons

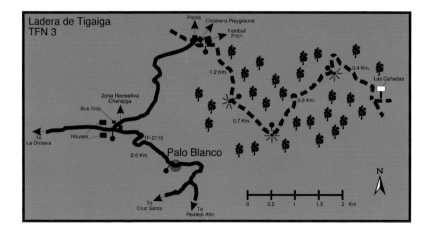

are most active. Bear in mind that there is often mist in this area.

Location:

From Santa Cruz: Take motorway TF-5 (Autopista del Norte) to the La Orotava/ Las Cañadas del Teide C-821 (Salida 17) exit. At the roundabout in La Orotava, turn left and go up the hill. Follow the signs for Parque Nacional del Teide and turn left onto C-821. After about 8 km, you will get to "Camino de Chasna" where you turn right onto TF-2115 to Palo Blanco/ Los Realejos. After 4.4 km and just after the 6 KM sign, turn left to "Zona Recreativa Chanajija", which is not signposted (Look for "Bar y Viveres Susana" on your right and a Bus stop on your left).
Carry on up this road up for 6.3 km, following the signs for "Zona Recreativa Chanajija". Turn left at Bar Casa Tomas, and then take the main fork to the right. At the T-junciton, turn right onto a dirt track that will lead you to the picnic area, playground and football pitch. To get to the laurel forest, stay on this dirt track.

From Puerto de la Cruz: Take motorway TF-5 (Autopista del Norte) to the Los Realejos (Por la Montañeta) TF-213 exit. Follow the signs for TF-213 La Montañeta/ Los Realejos. Enter La Zamora and turn left at the mini-roundabout to Cruz Santa (About 2.2 km from the motorway exit). You will pass Cruz Santa Reservoir on your right, and then turn right to Los Realejos. Turn left to La Cruz Santa/ Palo Blanco and then right again to "Salida Palo Blanco/Las Cañadas". Keep on TF-2115 to Palo Blanco/Las Cañadas and turn right to "Zona Recreativa Chanajija". Go up this road up for 6.3 km, following the signs for "Zona Recreativa Chanajija". At Bar Casa Tomas, turn left and then take the main fork to the right. At the T-junction, turn right onto the dirt track that leads to the picnic area, playground and football pitch. To get to the laurel forest, stay on this dirt track.

Laurel Pigeon

From Las Americas/ Los Cristianos: Take TF-1 to Santa Cruz and exit at Parque Nacional del Teide. Follow the signs for Vilaflor and Parque Nacional del Teide. Cross the National Park on the C-821 to la Orotava. 4.7 km past Aguamansa (or "Zona Recreativa la Caldera") turn left onto TF-2115 to Palo Blanco/ Los Realejos. Turn left after 4.4 km and the 6 KM sign, to "Zona Recreativa Chanajija", which is not signposted. (Look for "Bar y Viveres Susana" on your right and a bus stop on your left).
Stay on this road for 6.3 km, following the signs for "Zona Recreativa Chanajija". At Bar Casa Tomas, turn left and then take the main fork to the right. At the T-junction, turn right onto a dirt track that leads to the picnic area, playground and football pitch. To get to the laurel forest, stay on this dirt track.

Strategy:
The dirt track to the vantagepoints is in fairly good condition, but it is not recommended to follow the track all the way to the end as it gets rough and you need a 4WD vehicle.
The viewpoints and lookouts are excellent for observing the pigeons in flight as they allow you to view a large area. Always follow the pigeon with binoculars until it is out of sight. This is the only way to locate a bird that decides to perch on an exposed branch or rock.

Birds:
Year round: Sparrowhawk, Common Buzzard, Common Kestrel, Woodcock, Rock Dove, Bolle´s Pigeon, Laurel Pigeon, Plain Swift, Berthelot´s Pipit, Robin, Blackbird, Sardinian Warbler, Blackcap, Canary Islands Chiffchaff, Canary Islands Kinglet, Blue Tit, Chaffinch, Canary.
Summer visitors: Turtle Dove.

● CRUZ SANTA RESERVOIR   TFN4
Category: none
(Los Realejos Reservoir, Embalse de la Cruz Santa)

Description:
This is the largest concrete-banked, fenced reservoir in Tenerife, and is the best site for migrants in the north. A telescope is essential when visiting this site. The fields nearby are good for passerines and some endemic bird species.

Time to visit:
The best time to visit is during migration, but a winter visit could also be rewarding (September to June).

Location:
From Santa Cruz/ Puerto de la Cruz: Take motorway TF-5 (Autopista del Norte) to the Los Realejos (Por la Montañeta) TF-213 exit. Follow the signs for TF-213 La Montañeta/Los Realejos. Enter La Zamora and turn left at the mini-roundabout to Cruz Santa. (About 2.2 km from the motorway exit). Park at the lay-by on your right, about 0.7 km past the mini-roundabout. You will see the reservoir on your right.

From Las Americas/ Los Cristianos: Take TF-1 to Santa Cruz and exit at Parque Nacional del Teide. Follow the signs for Vilaflor and Parque Nacional del Teide.

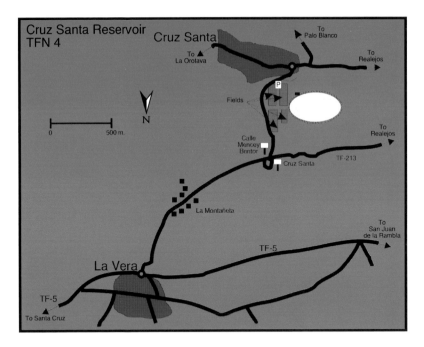

Cross the National Park on the C-821 to la Orotava and Puerto de la Cruz. Take TF-5 (Autopista del Norte) to the Los Realejos (Por la Montañeta) TF-213 exit. Follow the signs for TF-213 La Montañeta/Los Realejos. Enter La Zamora and turn left at the mini-roundabout to Cruz Santa. (About 2.2 km from the motorway exit). Park at the lay-by on your right, about 0.7 km from the mini-roundabout. You will see the reservoir on your right.

Strategy:
Scan the shores of the reservoir to look for birds.

Birds:
Year round: Little Egret, Grey Heron, Common Kestrel, Moorhen, Yellow-legged Gull, Rock Dove, Plain Swift, Hoopoe, Berthelot´s Pipit, Grey Wagtail, Blackbird, Spectacled Warbler, Sardinian Warbler, Blackcap, Canary Islands Chiffchaff, Blue Tit, Spanish Sparrow, Canary, Linnet.
Summer visitors: Turtle Dove, Pallid Swift.
Winter visitors: Wigeon, Common Teal, Pintail, Coot, Greenshank, Common Sandpiper, Black-headed Gull, Lesser Black-backed Gull, White Wagtail.
Passage migrants: Black-necked Grebe, Cattle Egret, White Stork, Spoonbill, Osprey, Lapwing, Swallow, House Martin.
Accidentals: Great Blue Heron*, Green-winged Teal, Black Duck*, Ring-necked Duck*, American Golden Plover*, Spotted Sandpiper*, Ring-billed Gull*.
(Passage migrants and accidental birds with an asterisk * have been accepted by the Spanish Rarities Committee, or have been recorded by the author).

● EL LANCE VIEWPOINT   TFN5
Category: none

Description:
This is just a lookout with a bar/restaurant, but is of interest for ornithologists as it is considered to be the most accessible site for Laurel Pigeon in Tenerife. Occassionally, it can be seen crossing this area on its way to the private cultivated fields near the coast where it feeds.

Time to visit:
You can visit this site all year round although the birds´ movements vary with the seasons.

Location:
From Santa Cruz/ Puerto de la Cruz: Take motorway TF-5 (Autopista del Norte) to the TF-1323 Los Realejos/ Puerto de la Cruz (Por las Dehesas) exit. Follow the signs for Los Realejos (town centre), and once in Los Realejos, go straight over at the first roundabout. Follow the sign for the "Centro de Salud". At the second roundabout turn right towards the church. The church will be on your left, and you pass the Town Hall on your right before turning right to Icod el Alto TF-221 (Mirador El Lance). Park after 4.8 km.

From Las Americas/ Los Cristianos: Take TF-1 to Santa Cruz and exit at Parque Nacional del Teide. Follow the signs for Vilaflor and Parque Nacional del Teide. Cross the National Park on C-821 to La Orotava and Puerto de la Cruz. Take TF-5 (Autopista del Norte) to the TF-1323 Los Realejos/ Puerto de la Cruz (Por las Dehesas) exit. Follow the signs for Los Realejos (town centre), and once in the town go straight over at the first roundabout. Follow the sign for the "Centro de Salud". At the second roundabout turn right towards the church. The church will be on your left, and you pass the Town Hall on your right before turning right to Icod el Alto TF-221 (Mirador El Lance). Park after 4.8 km.

Strategy:
Laurel Pigeon moves down towards the coast in the morning, returning in the afternoon. The time interval varies considerably, but this is the basic movement.

Birds:
Year round: Common Buzzard, Common Kestrel, Rock Dove, Laurel Pigeon, Plain Swift, Blackbird, Sardinian Warbler, Blackcap, Canary Islands Chiffchaff, Blue Tit, Spanish Sparrow, Canary.
Summer visitors: Turtle Dove, Pallid Swift.

● LA TABONA & BUEN PASO RESERVOIRS   TFN6
Category: none

Description:
These concrete-banked, fenced reservoirs are under-watched, but attract several migrants and are worth a quick look during migration. You can sometimes see Osprey fishing here.

TFN3 LADERA DE TIGAIGA

TFN4 CRUZ SANTA RESERVOIR

TFN2 LA CALDERA

TFN3 LADERA DE TIGAIGA

Time to visit:
The best times to visit are during migratory periods and in winter (September to June).

Location:
From Santa Cruz/ Puerto de la Cruz: Take motorway TF-5 (Autopista del Norte) to the TF-1323 Los Realejos/ Puerto de la Cruz (Por las Dehesas) exit. Follow the signs for Los Realejos (town centre), and once in the town, go straight over at the first roundabout. Follow the sign for the "Centro de Salud". At the second roundabout turn right towards the church. The church will be on your left, and you pass the Town Hall on your right before turning right to Icod el Alto TF-221 (Mirador El Lance). The "Mirador El Lance" is 4.8 km from this last turn. Stay on this road for 9.1 km and then turn right to "Embalse de la Tabona" near Bar/Restaurant El Pinalete. After 0.8 km, there is a lay-by on your right where you can park.
To get to Buen Paso, carry on for another 3.4 km from the junction where you turned right for "Embalse de la Tabona". Buen Paso will be on your left, and you can park near the gate.

From Las Americas/ Los Cristianos: Take TF-1 to Santa Cruz and exit at Parque Nacional del Teide. Follow the signs for Vilaflor and Parque Nacional del Teide. Cross the National Park on C-821 to la Orotava and Puerto de la Cruz. Take TF-5 (Autopista del Norte) to the TF-1323 Los Realejos/ Puerto de la Cruz (Por las Dehesas) exit. Follow the signs to Los Realejos (town centre), and once in the town, go straight over at the first roundabout. Follow the sign for the "Centro de Salud". At the second roundabout turn right towards the church. The church will be on your left, and you pass the Town Hall on your right before turning right to Icod el Alto TF-221 (Mirador El Lance). The "Mirador El Lance" is 4.8 km from this last turn. Stay on this road for 9.1 km and then turn right to "Embalse de la Tabona" near Bar/Restaurant El Pinalete. After 0.8 km, there is a lay-by on your right where you can park.
To get to Buen Paso, carry on for another 3.4 km from the junction where you turned right for "Embalse de la Tabona". Buen Paso will be on your left, and you can park near the gate.

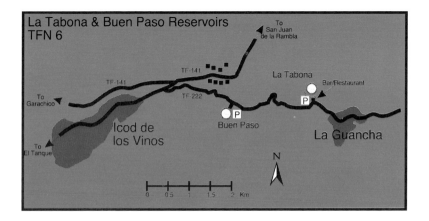

Strategy:
Scan the shores of the reservoir to look for migrants and check the trees for resident bird species.

Birds:
Year round: Little Egret, Grey Heron, Osprey, Common Kestrel, Yellow-legged Gull, Rock Dove, Plain Swift, Hoopoe, Berthelot´s Pipit, Grey Wagtail, Robin, Blackbird, Spectacled Warbler, Sardinian Warbler, Blackcap, Canary Islands Chiffchaff, Canary Islands Kinglet, Blue Tit, Spanish Sparrow, Chaffinch, Canary, Greenfinch, Linnet.
Summer visitors: Turtle Dove, Pallid Swift.
Winter visitors: Black-necked Grebe, Greenshank, Common Sandpiper.
Passage migrants: Black-necked Grebe*, Osprey*.
(Passage migrants with an asterisk * have been accepted by the Spanish Rarities Committee, or have been recorded by the author).

Canary

THE
NORTHEAST (TFNE)
Sections (1,2,3)

Bolle's Pigeon

THE NORTHEAST (TFNE)

This is a vast area with a range of important habitats, and due to the variety of information on each of these, this region has been divided into three different sections. The first section includes Santa Cruz, the boat trips that can be taken from here and the Rural Park of Anaga, one of the two ancient massifs on Tenerife. The second section deals mainly with the most important agricultural or cultivated areas in the Northeast and lists some important bird sites for migrants. The third section has a few interesting sites where it is possible to get good views of some endemics.

SECTION 1 (TFNE1)

Northeast 1 is characterised by the urban area of Santa Cruz (TFNE1.1) and the boat trips that can be taken from here (TFNE1.2, TFNE1.3, TFNE1.4). However, it also includes the Rural Park of Anaga (TFNE1.6, TFNE1.7, TFNE1.8) which holds the most extensive and undisturbed area of laurel forest on Tenerife.

All the birds generally associated with this type of habitat can be observed here although Laurel Pigeon is not as abundant and therefore difficult to catch sight of. However, this last fact could be the reason why Bolle´s Pigeon is so common in this area, and why it is not uncommon to see them perched here.

The Rural Park is a region of wooded "barrancos" (deep ravines or gorges) and is extremely humid, even during the summer months. Be prepared for this when you

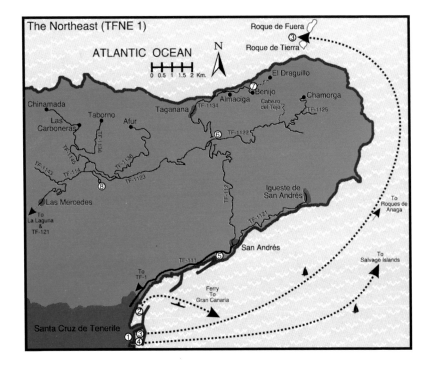

are planning your visit. Barbary Falcon breeds in the coastal cliffs near Benijo and can sometimes be observed near the Rural Park (TFNE1.7) although they can turn up anywhere, even in Santa Cruz port. This area is the only breeding ground on Tenerife for Madeiran Storm-petrel, and is only accessible by boat. Landing is prohibited at the Roques de Anaga (TFNE1.3).

● PLAZA DE LA CONCEPCION   TFNE1. 1
Category: none

Description:
A few small populations of various introduced species occur in and around this plaza.
Ring-necked Parakeet, Monk Parakeet and Common Myna have all been breeding feral for decades, and several other escapes from the city are also attracted to this site. Plaza de la Conception is very close to the Tenerife Natural History Museum, which is worth a visit.

Time to visit:
This area is good for visiting all year round.

Location:
From Puerto de la Cruz: Take motorway TF-5 to Santa Cruz (Avenida Maritima). Turn left into Avenida de José Antonio Primo de Rivera. Take the first left into Avenida de Bravo Murillo, just next to the Hacienda building and then turn right. The site is on your left before the next traffic lights.

From Las Americas/ Los Cristianos: Take motorway TF-1 to Santa Cruz (Avenida Maritima). Go past the entrance to the port (Muelle) and you will be on Avenida de José Antonio Primo de Rivera. Turn left at the Hacienda building into Avenida de Bravo Murillo where you should turn right. The site is on your left before the next traffic lights.

Strategy:
Walk around the plaza checking the tile roofs and the main tower for mynas. You can usually see the Parakeets in the trees along the main street (Avenida de Bravo Murillo).

Birds:
Year round: Common Kestrel, Yellow-legged Gull, Rock Dove, Collared Dove, Ring-necked Parakeet, Monk Parakeet, Plain Swift, Grey Wagtail, Blackbird, Blackcap, Canary Islands Chiffchaff, Spanish Sparrow.
Summer visitors: Turtle Dove, Pallid Swift.
Winter visitors: Barbary Falcon, Starling.
Escapes: Red-cheeked Cordon-Blue, Red-headed Cardinal, Amazon Parrot.

● FERRY TO GRAN CANARIA   TFNE1. 2
Category: none

Description:
The ferry crossing to Gran Canaria provides excellent opportunities for seawatching. It departs from Santa Cruz.

Time to visit:
Late August, early September is the best time to take this ferry as interesting seabirds are passing through and the Canarian specialities are still present (Bulwer´s Petrel, Cory´s Shearwater, Little Shearwater). April is another good month for passing seabirds.

Location:
From Puerto de la Cruz: Take motorway TF-5 to Santa Cruz (Avenida Maritima). Follow the signs for "El Muelle". Tell the guards you are taking the ferry. Once you enter the harbour, the companies operating to Gran Canaria are on your right.

From Las Americas/ Los Cristianos: Take motorway TF-1 to Santa Cruz (Avenida Maritima). Follow the signs for "El Muelle". Tell the guards you are taking the Ferry. Once you enter the harbour, the two companies operating to Gran Canaria are on your right.

Little Shearwater

Strategy:
The best views are obtained by staying as close to the bow as possible.

Birds:
Year round: Little Shearwater, Yellow-legged Gull.
Summer visitors: Bulwer´s Petrel, Cory´s Shearwater, Manx Shearwater, Common Tern.
Winter visitors: Grey Phalarope, Black-headed Gull, Lesser Black-backed Gull, Sandwich Tern.
Passage migrants: Great Shearwater*, Manx Shearwater*, Grey Phalarope*, Great Skua*, Arctic Tern*.
Accidentals: Sooty Shearwater*.
(Passage migrants and accidental birds with an asterisk * have been accepted by the Spanish Rarities Committee, or have been recorded by the author).

Other wildlife:
Fish: Tropical Two-winged Flyingfish (*Exocoetus volitans*), Oceanic Two-winged Flyingfish (*Exocoetus obtusirostris*), Bennett´s Flyingfish (*Cypselurus pinnatibarbatus*).
Reptiles: Loggerhead Turtle.
Cetaceans: Short-finned Pilot Whale, Bottlenose Dolphin.

● **BOAT TRIP TO ROQUES DE ANAGA**   **TFNE1. 3**
Category: Integral Nature Reserve

Description:
This very important Nature Reserve is characterised by two islets off the north coast of Tenerife. The closest to Tenerife, Roque de Dentro (inward islet), is 179 metres high and lies some 300 metres from the main island. It is, in actual fact, connected to Tenerife. Roque de Fuera (outward islet) is larger and lies about 1.5 km from Tenerife. Both have some vegetation, and a resident colony of Yellow-legged Gull. It is forbidden to land on either of the islets as they are breeding grounds for some of the most important seabirds in the Archipelago. The waters

surrounding the reserve are the best place to look for Madeiran Storm-petrel in autumn and winter.

Time to visit:
Late September to February are the best times to look for Madeiran Storm-petrel, but due to bad weather conditions, December to Februray should be avoided.

*Madeiran
Storm-petrel*

Location:
From Puerto de la Cruz: Take motorway TF-5 to Santa Cruz (Avenida Maritima). Follow the signs for "El Muelle". Tell the guards you are going to "Marina del Atlantico", which will be on your right after "Naviera Armas".

From Las Americas/ Los Cristianos: Take motorway TF-1 to Santa Cruz (Avenida Maritima). Follow the signs for "El Muelle". Tell the guards you are going to "Marina del Atlantico", which will be on your right after "Naviera Armas".

Strategy:
It is advisable to set off as early as possible to get the best views of the birds. It will take about 4 hours to get to the reserve, going at a speed of around 4-6 knots. Tell the skipper to sail straight to Roques de Anaga and to head for Punta del Hidalgo once you get to the islets.
If you are interested in chartering a yacht, please contact:

AVES ECOTOURS S.L.
C/ Fernando Barajas Vilchez 9
38004 Santa Cruz de Tenerife
Canary Islands
Spain
Tel: (00 34) 922 27 99 58
Tel: (00 34) 922 22 17 50
Fax: (00 34) 922 22 16 69
E-mail: avesecot@redkbs.com

Birds:
Year round: Little Shearwater, Yellow-legged Gull.
Summer visitors: Bulwer´s Petrel, Cory´s Shearwater, European Storm-petrel, Common Tern.
Winter breeders: Madeiran Storm-petrel.
Winter visitors: Black-headed Gull, Lesser Black-backed Gull, Sandwich Tern.

Other wildlife:
Reptiles: Loggerhead Turtle, Green Turtle.
Cetaceans: Short-finned Pilot Whale, Bottlenose Dolphin.

● BOAT TRIP TO SALVAGES   TFNE1. 4
Category: Nature Reserve belonging to Portugal

Description:
This remote Archipelago is made up of two main islands and a few islets and rocks. Salvage Pequeña (small Salvage) is the closest to Tenerife and has the lowest

elevation. Large numbers of White-faced Storm-petrel
breed on this island. Salvage Grande, which is
situated a little way to the north, covers a bigger
area and has a higher altitude. The Salvages lie
some 70 miles from Tenerife, and it takes about
17-20 hours by yacht at a speed of 6-7 knots.
You are not allowed to land on the islands, and
it is not necessary as the birds can be observed
easily from the boat.

Time to visit:
The best time to visit the Salvage Islands is
between June and September.

Location:
From Puerto de la Cruz: Take motorway TF-5 to Santa Cruz
(Avenida Maritima). Follow the signs for "El Muelle". Tell
the guards you are going to "Marina del Atlantico", which will
be on your right after "Naviera Armas".

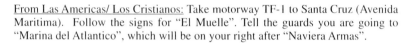

*White-face
Storm-petre*

From Las Americas/ Los Cristianos: Take motorway TF-1 to Santa Cruz (Avenida
Maritima). Follow the signs for "El Muelle". Tell the guards you are going to
"Marina del Atlantico", which will be on your right after "Naviera Armas".

Strategy:
If you are interested in chartering a yacht, please contact:

AVES ECOTOURS S.L.
C/ Fernando Barajas Vilchez 9
38004 Santa Cruz de Tenerife
Canary Islands
Spain

The best way to see White-faced Strom-petrel is to sail round the northern waters of
Salvage Pequeña at dusk although they can occur virtually anywhere. This time of
day is good as they can be seen coming ashore to their burrows. Beware of the
rocky reefs surrounding Salvage Pequeña.

Birds:
Year round: Little Shearwater, Kestrel, Yellow-legged Gull, Berthelot´s Pipit.
Summer visitors: Bulwer´s Petrel, Cory´s Shearwater, White-faced Storm-petrel,
Madeiran Storm-petrel, Common Tern.
Passage Migrants: Wilson´s Storm-petrel, Pomarine Skua, Arctic Skua, Sabine´s
Gull.
Accidentals: Swinhoe´s Storm-petrel, Eleonora´s Falcon, Sooty Tern, Collared Dove,
Crag Martin, Swallow, Red-rumped Swallow, Whinchat, Grasshopper Warbler,
Olivaceous Warbler, Icterine Warbler, Red-backed Shrike, Siskin, Yellow Warbler,
American Redstart.

Other wildlife:
Fish: Shark.
Reptiles: Loggerhead Turtle, Green Turtle.
Cetaceans: Short-finned Pilot Whale, Bottlenose Dolphin.

● DARSENA PESQUERA   TFNE1. 5
Category: none
(Fishing Quay)

Description:
This is a fishing port with a resident colony of Yellow-legged Gull. The surrounding fields are gradually becoming more and more developed, and unfortunately this site could loose its potential in the not so distant future.

Time to visit:
A winter visit could be rewarding.

Location:
From Puerto de la Cruz: Take motorway TF-5 to Santa Cruz, and follow the signs for Avenida Maritima. At the main traffic lights turn left onto Avenida Jose Antonio Primo de Rivera. Follow this road along the coast until it becomes TF-111. Follow the signs for "Darsena Pesquera".

From Las Americas/ Los Cristianos: Take motorway TF-1 to Santa Cruz, following the signs for Avenida Maritima, which will bring you onto Avenida Jose Antonio Primo de Rivera. Follow this road along the coast until it becomes TF-111. Follow the signs for "Darsena Pesquera".

Strategy:
Check the gulls on the quayside.

Birds:
Year round: Yellow-legged Gull.
Summer visitors: Common Tern.
Winter visitors: Lesser Black-backed Gull, Sandwich Tern.
Passage migrants: Common Tern*, Arctic Tern*.
Accidentals: Common Gull, Bar-tailed Desert Lark*.
(Passage migrants and accidental birds with an asterisk * have been accepted by the Spanish Rarities Committee, or have been recorded by the author).

● El BAILADERO & CABEZA DEL TEJO   TFNE1. 6
Category: Anaga Rural Park

Description:
This is a wooded area of monteverde (a mixture of laurel forest and fayal-brezal). You can get excellent views of the endemic subspecies of Chaffinch from the fields to the south, just near the restaurant and bar at El Bailadero. Other interesting birds can also be observed here, but it is worth a visit just to admire the scenery.

Time to visit:
You can visit this site all year round, but try to avoid winter when it is normally misty and windy.

Location:
From Santa Cruz/ Las Americas/ Los Cristianos: Take motorway TF-1 to Santa Cruz (Avenida Maritima). Follow the road along the coast until you find yourself on TF-111 to San Andrés. Turn left onto TF-112 towards El Bailadero and Taganana.

"Do not turn right to Taganana". After 2 km turn right to El Bailadero (TF-1122), where you will find a place to park near the bar after some 400 metres. Continue until you reach the dirt track to Cabeza del Tejo.

From Puerto de la Cruz/ La Laguna: Take motorway TF-5 to the La Laguna exit. Follow the signs for Monte de las Mercedes, which will lead you onto TF-114. Take TF-114 to TF-1123 and turn left to El Bailadero (TF-1122). You can park near the bar at El Bailadero. Continue until you reach the dirt track to Cabeza del Tejo.

Strategy:
The dirt track to Cabeza del Tejo is in good condition, but a 4WD is recommended. The viewpoint is at the end of the track, and is good for Bolle´s Pigeon and other birds associated with this type of forest. Keep both eyes open for Barbary Falcon. The scenery is just spectacular although the weather is often windy and foggy.

Birds:
Year round: Sparrowhawk, Common Buzzard, Common Kestrel, Barbary Falcon, Woodcock, Rock Dove, Bolle´s Pigeon, Plain Swift, Grey Wagtail, Robin, Blackbird, Sardinian Warbler, Blackcap, Canary Islands Chiffchaff, Canary Islands Kinglet, Blue Tit, Chaffinch, Canary.
Summer visitors: Turtle Dove.
Passage migrants: Swallow, House Martin.

● BENIJO   TFNE1. 7
Category: Anaga Rural Park

Description:
This is a very small village located at the end of the road to Taganana. Take the track that heads eastwards, bearing in mind that you really need a 4WD here. This area is good for Barbary Falcon, and also very good for seawatching. Avoid bad weather conditions as the track can get slippery and dangerous.

Time to visit:
May to September is good for seawatching. Any time during the year should produce the Falcon.

Location:
From Santa Cruz/ Las Americas/ Los Cristianos: Take motorway TF-1 to Santa Cruz (Avenida Maritima). Follow the road along the coast, which becomes TF-111 to San Andrés. Turn left onto TF-112 towards El Bailadero and Taganana. Turn right to Taganana (TF-1134) and go through the town to reach Benijo. Park near the bar/restaurant.

From Puerto de la Cruz/ La Laguna: Take motorway TF-5 to the La Laguna exit. Follow the signs for Monte de las Mercedes and turn onto TF-114. Take TF-114 to TF-1123 and turn left to Taganana (TF-1134). Go through the town to reach Benijo. Park near the bar/restaurant.

Strategy:
The rough track to El Draguillo is not in good condition and can also be dangerous, so be very careful if entering this area.

Birds:
<u>Year round:</u> Yellow-legged Gull, Sparrowhawk, Common Buzzard, Common Kestrel, Barbary Falcon, Woodcock, Rock Dove, Plain Swift, Grey Wagtail, Robin, Blackbird, Sardinian Warbler, Blackcap, Canary Islands Chiffchaff, Blue Tit, Canary.
<u>Summer visitors:</u> Cory´s Shearwater, Turtle Dove.

● MONTE DE LAS MERCEDES & PICO DEL INGLES   TFNE1. 8
Category: Anaga Rural Park

Description:
The windy road through this wooded region provides access to a few lookouts and picnic areas that are good for some endemic bird species and subspecies.
The picnic area at Monte de las Mercedes is very good for Chaffinch, Robin and the ocassional Kinglet. Bolle´s Pigeon can be heard calling early in the day, but they are very hard to see here.
Pico del Ingles (Englishman´s Peak) is a good spot for observing Bolle´s Pigeon in flight. In the hotter summer months Laurel Pigeon has been seen in this area. Barbary Falcon and Pallid Swift have also been recorded at this lookout.

Time to visit:
Any time during the year is good for visiting this site, but the summer months are best if you are looking for Laurel Pigeon. It is worth noting that any of the sites in this area are extremely prone to dense cloud and fog throughout the year.

Location:
<u>From Santa Cruz/ Las Americas/ Los Cristianos:</u> Take motorway TF-1 to TF-5 (Autopista del Norte) towards La Laguna. Exit at La Laguna/ Via de Ronda. Follow the sings for Via de Ronda. Keep on to Las Canteras/Tegueste (TF-121) passing over the first roundabout and going right at the second. Follow the signs for Monte de las Mercedes (TF-114) and turn left into the picnic area. Stay on this road to get to Pico del Inglés.

<u>From Puerto de la Cruz/ La Laguna:</u> Take motorway TF-5 to the La Laguna (Por San Benito (Salida 26) exit. Follow the signs for Monte de las Mercedes (TF-114) and turn left into the picnic area. Stay on this road to get to Pico del Inglés.

Strategy:
The viewpoints are excellent for observing the pigeons in flight as you cover a wide area. Always follow the pigeon with binoculars until it is no longer in sight. This is the only way to locate a bird that decides to perch on an exposed branch or rock.

Birds:
<u>Year round:</u> Sparrowhawk, Common Buzzard, Common Kestrel, Barbary Falcon, Woodcock, Rock Dove, Bolle´s Pigeon, Laurel Pigeon, Plain Swift, Grey Wagtail, Robin, Blackbird, Sardinian Warbler, Blackcap, Canary Islands Chiffchaff, Canary Islands Kinglet, Blue Tit, Chaffinch, Canary.
<u>Summer visitors:</u> Turtle Dove, Pallid Swift.

SECTION 2 (TFNE2)

The agricultural land near the airport in the North, "Los Rodeos" (TFNE2.2), is the best site to look for Quail in Tenerife. At night, you can also find the two species of owl that occur in the Canary Islands hunting together. This agricultural area is also good for migrants and some interesting wintering bird species. An interesting subspecies of Lesser Short-toed Lark (*rufescens ssp.*) can be seen in Los Rodeos area although it is becoming very rare.

A fairly good population of Serin breed around La Laguna (TFNE2.1), and there are also some very good migrant sites to the north: (TFNE2.4, TFNE2.5, TFNE2.6, TFNE2.7).

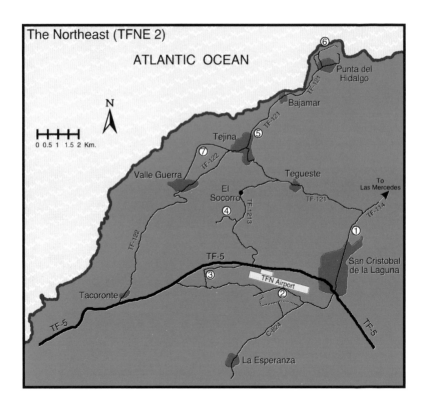

● **LA LAGUNA**   **TFNE2. 1**
  Category: none

Description:
The trees are excellent for finches, up to five different species can be seen feeding together amidst the foliage. Sometimes there can be a few identification problems here as Serin and Canary can often be observed together.

Time to visit:
Spring is the best time to look for the finches as they will be breeding and more active. Try to get to the site by early morning or visit late in the afternoon.

Location:
From Santa Cruz: Take motorway TF-1 to TF-5 (Autopista del Norte) towards La Laguna. Exit at La Laguna/ Via de Ronda and follow the signs for Via de Ronda. At the first roundabout turn left and park on the dirt track about 1km along.

Strategy:
Walk along the road listening out for the call of the Serin and other finches. The small stream or channel is good for Grey Wagtail.

Birds:
Year round: Sparrowhawk, Common Buzzard, Common Kestrel, Rock Dove, Barn Owl, Plain Swift, Grey Wagtail, Blackbird, Blackcap, Canary Islands Chiffchaff, Blue Tit, Starling, Spanish Sparrow, Serin, Canary, Greenfinch, Goldfinch, Linnet. Summer visitors: Turtle Dove, Pallid Swift.
Winter visitors: Starling.

● **LOS RODEOS AIRPORT**   **TFNE2. 2**
Category: Important Bird Area (IBA)

Description:
This area of cultivated plains and scattered eucaliptus trees is very good for Quail

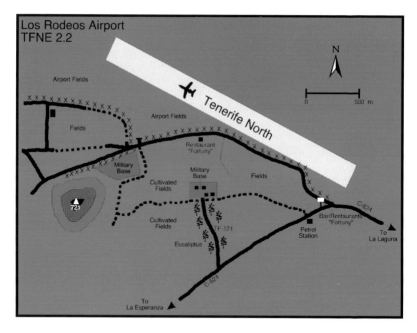

although it is more often heard than seen. The size of the crops determines their ornithological potential. Quail is more common in the tall grass whereas Lesser Short-toed Lark favours the arid rock with its sparse vegetation. At night, the airport provides enough light to go owling without a flashlight, and you can see the owls perched on the airport fences.

Time to visit:
Spring is the best time to visit this site although a winter visit could also be rewarding. September to November and February to April are the best times for migrants. Avoid winter months if looking for owls.

Location:
From Santa Cruz: Take motorway TF-5 (Autopista del Norte) to the La Laguna and Parque Nacional del Teide exit. Turn left and go past the roundabout, following the signs for La Esperanza (C-824) and Parque Nacional del Teide. 1.4 km after the roundabout, turn right onto the road parallel to the airport fence which is signposted "Bar/restaurante Fortuny" and "Perez Ortega". Park in any of the lay-bys on the left-hand side of the road, about 0.7km from where you turned off.

From Puerto de la Cruz: Take motorway TF-5 (Autopista del Norte) to the La Laguna/Las Cañadas/Geneto exit ("Do not take La Laguna (Por San Benito) Salida 26"). At the roundabout turn right to La Esperanza (C-824) and Parque Nacional del Teide. 1.4 km after the roundabout, turn right onto the road parallel to the airport fence which is signposted "Bar/restaurante Fortuny" and "Perez Ortega". Park in any of the lay-bys on the left- hand side of the road about 0.7km from where you turned off.

Strategy:
Check the cultivated fields with tall vegetation for Quail and listen out for their

typical tri-syllabic call "Wet-my-lips". The best way to locate the Lesser Short-toed Lark is also by their call or song as they circle above. Check the fields on either side of the airport and especially the first 0.7 km of the airport road. The traffic tends to move very-fast along this stretch of road, so be careful. If you are visiting this site at night check the airport fence to look for both species of owls.

Birds:
Year round: Sparrowhawk, Common Buzzard, Common Kestrel, Quail, Rock Dove, Barn Owl, Long-eared Owl, Plain Swift, Lesser Short-toed Lark (*rufescens*), Berthelot´s Pipit, Grey Wagtail, Blackbird, Spectacled Warbler, Sardinian Warbler, Blackcap, Canary Islands Chiffchaff, Blue Tit, Spanish Sparrow, Canary, Greenfinch, Goldfinch, Linnet, Corn Bunting.

Long-eared Owl

Summer visitors: Turtle Dove, Pallid Swift.
Winter visitors: European Golden Plover, Lapwing, Short-eared Owl, Stonechat, Starling.
Passage migrants: Marsh Harrier*, Hen Harrier*, Montagu´s Harrier*, Collared Pratincole, Dotterel, Cuckoo*, Short-toed Lark, Swallow*, House Martin*, Tawny Pipit, Meadow Pipit, Red-throated Pipit, Black-eared Wheatear, Great Reed Warbler, Willow Warbler, Woodchat Shrike.
Accidentals: Pallid Harrier*, Great Spotted Cuckoo, Desert Wheatear.
(Passage migrants and accidental birds with an asterisk * have been accepted by the Spanish Rarities Committee, or have been recorded by the author).

● **EL PEÑON GOLF COURSE**   **TFNE2. 3**
Category: none

Description:
This is a golf course in the North, which is worth a quick look if passing by during migratory periods. Although under-watched, it is a good site for Greenfinch and Serin, two finches which are not widely distributed on Tenerife. Crossbill has also been recorded in the area.

Time to visit:
Spring is the best time to look for resident passerines (finches and others), and the best months for migrants are September to November and February to June. The winter months are best for Siskin.

Location:
From Santa Cruz/ La Laguna: Take motorway TF-5 (Autopista del Norte) to the Los Rodeos exit. Turn right onto a secondary road that runs parallel to the motorway (Do not cross the bridge to the airport). Turn left to Tegueste (TF-1213) and stay on this road until you see the sign "Campo de Golf". Follow this sign until you enter the golf course. Park in the golf course car park.

From Puerto de la Cruz: Take motorway TF-5 (Autopista del Norte) to the Guamasa exit. Follow the signs for "Campo de Golf". Park in the golf course car park.

Strategy:
Walk the 18th hole until you get to a T-junction. Turn left to reach the fields where Quail breeds in spring.

Birds:
Year round: Sparrowhawk, Common Kestrel, Quail, Rock Dove, Barn Owl, Long-eared Owl, Plain Swift, Berthelot´s Pipit, Grey Wagtail, Blackbird, Spectacled Warbler, Sardinian Warbler, Blackcap, Canary Islands Chiffchaff, Canary Islands Kinglet, Blue Tit, Spanish Sparrow, Serin, Canary, Greenfinch, Linnet, Corn Bunting.
Summer visitors: Turtle Dove, Pallid Swift.
Winter visitors: White Wagtail, Siskin.
Passage migrants: Whimbrel.
Accidentals: Crossbill.

● VALLE MOLINA RESERVOIR   TFNE2. 4
Category: none
(Embalse de Valle Molina)

Description:
This concrete-banked, fenced reservoir is well located to attract migrants during passage and also some wintering bird species. The surrounding scrubby habitat is good for Plain Swift, Canary Islands Chiffchaff, Canary and Sardinian Warbler. Quail can sometimes be heard in spring.

Time to visit:
Anytime from September to June should be rewarding.

Location:
From Santa Cruz/ La Laguna: Take motorway TF-5 (Autopista del Norte) to the Aeropuerto/Los Rodeos exit. Turn right onto a secondary road that runs parallel to the motorway. (Do not cross the bridge to the airport). Turn left to Tegueste (TF-1213) and follow this road, passing a petrol station on your right. Turn right to Tegueste (Por el Socorro) TF-1213 and left after 3.4 km onto Camino de Valle Molina. You will see a bar/restaurant on your right. Park about 200 metres on to view the reservoir.

From Puerto de la Cruz: Take motorway TF-5 (Autopista del Norte) to Aeropuerto TFE-NORTE exit. Turn right, then right again at the roundabout. Pass the bridge, but keep going straight. Turn left to Tegueste (TF-1213) and follow this road, passing a petrol station on your right. Turn right to Tegueste (Por el Socorro) TF-1213 and left after 3.4 km onto Camino de Valle Molina. You will see a bar/restaurant on your right. Park about 200 metres on to view the reservoir.

Strategy :
Check the shores of the reservoir with a telescope.

Birds:
Year round: Little Egret, Grey Heron, Sparrowhawk, Common Buzzard, Common Kestrel, Barbary Falcon, Quail, Moorhen, Little Ringed Plover, Yellow-legged Gull, Rock Dove, Plain Swift, Grey Wagtail, Robin, Blackbird, Sardinian Warbler, Blackcap, Canary Islands Chiffchaff, Blue Tit, Spanish Sparrow, Serin, Canary, Greenfinch.

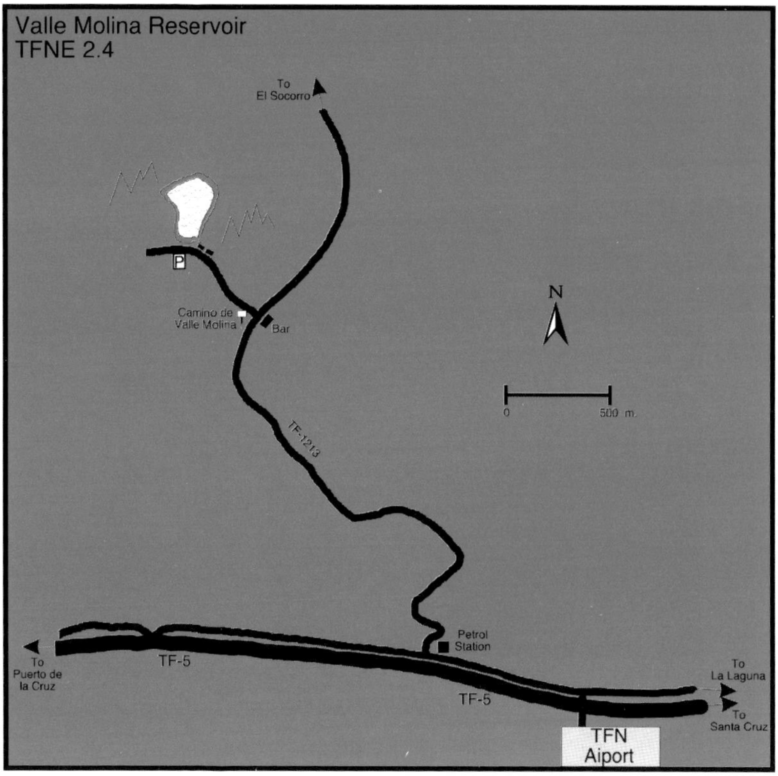

Summer visitors: Turtle Dove, Pallid Swift.
Winter visitors: Cattle Egret, Spoonbill, Wigeon, Common Teal, Pintail, Coot, Lapwing, Common Snipe, Greenshank, Green Sandpiper, Common Sandpiper, Black-headed Gull, White Wagtail, Siskin.
Passage migrants: Cattle Egret*, Spoonbill*, Wigeon, Gadwall*, Shoverler, Pochard, Tufted Duck*, Collared Pratincole, Grey Plover, Lapwing*, Knot*, Ruff*, Common Snipe*, Black-tailed Godwit, Wood Sandpiper*, Whiskered Tern*, Sand Martin*, Swallow*, House Martin*, Blue-headed Wagtail, Yellow Wagtail*.
Accidentals: Green-winged Teal*, Blue-winged Teal*, Ring-necked Duck*, Ring-billed Gull*.
(Passage migrants and accidental birds with an asterisk * have been accepted by the Spanish Rarities Committee, or have been recorded by the author).

● TEJINA PONDS — TFNE2. 5

Category: none
(Charcas de Tejina)

Description:
This is a very interesting site for migrants and wintering species. The tall vegetation round the edges of the six ponds provides shelter for the birds, and this is where Moorhen breeds and where Little Bittern has bred in the past.

Time to visit:
The best time is during migration, September to November and February to June.
A winter visit could also be rewarding.

Location:
From Santa Cruz: Take motorway TF-5 (Autopista del Norte) to the La Laguna/Via
de Ronda exit. Follow the signs for Via de Ronda and continue on to Las Canteras/
Tegueste TF-121. Pass Las Canteras and turn left to Tegueste/Punta del Hidalgo
TF-121. Once in Tejina, follow the signs for Bajamar/Punta del Hidalgo (TF-121).
To reach the first two ponds (A), park at Bar El Puente on your right about 600
metres after the turn. The next main pond (B) is 0.7 km from Bar El Puente, on
your left. You should be able to find a small path leading through the canes. Stay
on the road for a further 0.4 km to reach the other ponds (C) and the trail to the last
one (D).

From Puerto de la Cruz:
Take motorway TF-5 (Autopista del Norte) to the Aeropuerto TFE-NORTE exit.
Turn right, then right again at the roundabout. Pass the bridge, and keep going
straight. Turn left to Tegueste (TF-1213) and follow this road, passing a petrol station

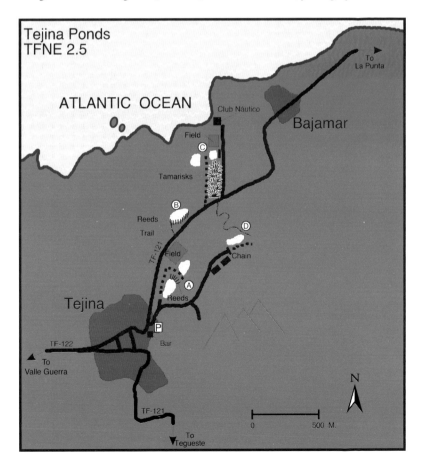

on your right. Turn right to Tegueste (Por el Socorro) TF-1213, and stay on this road until you reach the main road Tegueste-Tejina. Turn left and head for Tejina. Once in Tejina, follow the signs for Bajamar/Punta del Hidalgo (TF-121). To reach the first two ponds (A), park at Bar El Puente on your right about 600 metres after the turn. The next main pond (B) is 0.7 km from Bar El Puente, on your left. You should be able to find a small path leading through the canes. Stay on the road for a further 0.4 km to reach the other ponds (C) and the trail to the last one (D).

Strategy:
When checking the ponds, be as quiet as possible as birds might be flushed by your presence. Take the trail at (A) to get a better view of the area. The fields on the northern side often attract migrants.
There is a small path to the west leading to pond (B). Check the reeds and canes and the edges carefully. The smaller ponds at (C) do not attract many migrants, but are worth a quick look, just in case. The last pond (D) can be reached by road (see sketch), but as this is a private area, it is advisable to walk up the trail.

Birds:
Year round: Little Egret, Grey Heron, Sparrowhawk, Common Buzzard, Common Kestrel, Barbary Falcon, Barbary Partridge, Moorhen, Coot, Yellow-legged Gull, Rock Dove, Collared Dove, Long-eared Owl, Plain Swift, Grey Wagtail, Blackbird, Spectacled Warbler, Sardinian Warbler, Blackcap, Canary Islands Chiffchaff, Blue Tit, Spanish Sparrow, Canary, Greenfinch, Goldfinch, Linnet.
Summer visitors: Little Bittern, Turtle Dove, Pallid Swift.
Winter visitors: Coot, Common Snipe, Greenshank, Common Sandpiper, Black Redstart.
Passage migrants: Little Bittern, Night Heron*, Squacco Heron*, Cattle Egret*, Purple Heron*, White Stork, Spoonbill*, Wigeon*, Common Teal, Shoveler, Tufted Duck*, Marsh Harrier, Osprey, Spotted Crake*, Little Crake*, Baillon´s Crake*, Little Ringed Plover*, Lapwing*, Curlew Sandpiper*, Dunlin*, Ruff*, Common Snipe*, Black-tailed Godwit*, Wood Sandpiper, Common Sandpiper, Cuckoo, Common Swift*, European Bee-eater, Sand Martin*, Swallow*, Red-rumped Swallow*, House Martin*, Common Redstart*, Stonechat*, Northern Wheatear*, Sedge Warbler*, Great Reed Warbler*, Willow Warbler*, Woodchat Shrike*.
Accidentals: Bittern*, Scaup, Crag Martin.
Escapes: Hill Myna, Zebra Finch.
(Passage migrants and accidental birds with an asterisk * have been accepted by the Spanish Rarities Committee, or have been recorded by the author).

● **LA PUNTA**   **TFNE2. 6**
Category: none
(Punta del Hidalgo)

Description:
This is just about the most northerly point on Tenerife and sometimes good for seawatching. The coastal rocky shore provides an intertidal zone exposed at low tide, which is good for waders and terns in winter. This site used to be excellent for passerine migrants, but unfortunately recent development has destroyed the potential of this place.

Time to visit:
Spring is the best time to look for migrants (February to June), but most waders are

only present in the winter months at low tide (December to February). August and September are good for seawatching.

Location:
From Santa Cruz: Take motorway TF-5 (Autopista del Norte) to the La Laguna/Via de Ronda exit. Follow the signs for Via de Ronda, continuing on to Las Canteras/Tegueste TF-121. Pass Las Canteras and turn left to Tegueste/Punta del Hidalgo TF-121. Once in Tejina, follow the signs for Bajamar/Punta del Hidalgo (TF-121). Stay on this road until you reach La Punta. Turn left at the sign marked "Camping, then right onto the coastal track.

From Puerto de la Cruz:
Take motorway TF-5 (Autopista del Norte) to the Aeropuerto TFE-NORTE exit. Turn right and right again at the roundabout. Pass the bridge, but keep straight on. Turn left to Tegueste (TF-1213) and follow this road, passing a petrol station on your right. Turn right to Tegueste (Por el Socorro) TF-1213, and stay on this road until you reach the main Tegueste-Tejina road. Turn left to Tejina. Once in Tejina, follow the signs to Bajamar/Punta del Hidalgo (TF-121). Stay on this road until you reach La Punta. Turn left at the sign marked "Camping", and then right onto the coastal track.

Strategy:
A telescope is essential for seawatching.

Birds:
Year round: Little Egret, Grey Heron, Sparrowhawk, Common Buzzard, Common Kestrel, Yellow-legged Gull, Rock Dove, Long-eared Owl, Plain Swift, Hoopoe, Berthelot´s Pipit, Grey Wagtail, Blackbird, Spectacled Warbler, Sardinian Warbler, Blackcap, Canary Islands Chiffchaff, Blue Tit, Spanish Sparrow, Canary, Linnet.
Summer visitors: Cory´s Shearwater, Turtle Dove, Pallid Swift.
Winter visitors: Ringed Plover, Grey Plover, Whimbrel, Greenshank, Common Sandpiper, Turnstone, Sandwich Tern.
Passage migrants: Alpine Swift, European Bee-eater*, Short-toed Lark, Sand Martin, Swallow*, Red-rumped Swallow, House Martin, Tawny Pipit*, Red-throated Pipit, White Wagtail, Yellow Wagtail, Northern Wheatear, Melodious Warbler, Subalpine Warbler, Wood Warbler, Woodchat Shirke.
Accidentals: Purple Sandpiper*, Calandra Lark, Desert Wheatear*, Orphean Warbler, Red-breasted Flycatcher*.
(Passage migrants and accidental birds with an asterisk * have been accepted by the Spanish Rarities Committee, or have been recorded by the author).

● **LA BARRANQUERA RESERVOIRS**   **TFNE2. 7**
Category: none

Description:
This is a very fragmented area with a few reservoirs. The most interesting of these are four reservoirs in a small gully or *barranco*. The vegetation provides shelter for interesting migrants, and Little Bittern has also been recorded here. A small population of Moorhen breeds in the area.

Time to visit:
Spring migration is the best time to look for migrants (February to June).

Location:
From Santa Cruz: Take motorway TF-5 (Autopista del Norte) to the La Laguna/Via de Ronda exit. Follow the signs for Via de Ronda and continue on to Las Canteras/ Tegueste TF-121. Pass Las Canteras and turn left to Tegueste/Punta del Hidalgo TF-121. Once in Tejina, turn left at the roundabout to Valle Guerra/Tacoronte TF-122. Take the second right onto Camino de la Costa (you will see a petrol station on your left) and turn left at the first stop sign. Follow this road and turn right to La Barranquera TF-1221. Park after about 1.3 km near the dirt track to your right.

From Puerto de la Cruz:
Take motorway TF-5 (Autopista del Norte) to the Aeropuerto TFE-NORTE exit. Turn right and right again at the roundabout. Pass the bridge, but keep going straight. Turn left to Tegueste (TF-1213) and follow this road, passing a petrol station on your right. Turn right to Tegueste (Por el Socorro) TF-1213, and stay on this road until you reach the main Tegueste-Tejina road. Turn left and follow this road to Tejina. Once in Tejina, go left at the roundabout to Valle Guerra/Tacoronte F-122. Take the second right onto Camino de la Costa (you will see a petrol station on your left) and turn left at the first stop sign. Follow this road and turn right to La Barranquera TF-1221. Park after about 1.3 km near the dirt track to your right.

Strategy:
Follow the one-way dirt track to reach the reservoirs. Check the vegetation (canes) in each reservoir.

Birds:
Year round: Little Egret, Grey Heron, Sparrowhawk, Common Kestrel, Moorhen, Coot, Little Ringed Plover, Yellow-legged Gull, Rock Dove, Plain Swift, Hoopoe, Berthelot´s Pipit, Grey Wagtail, Blackbird, Spectacled Warbler, Sardinian Warbler, Blackcap, Canary Islands Chiffchaff, Blue Tit, Spanish Sparrow, Canary, Greenfinch, Goldfinch, Linnet.
Summer visitors: Turtle Dove, Pallid Swift.
Winter visitors: Coot, Common Sandpiper, White Wagtail.
Passage migrants: Little Bittern*, Night Heron*, Squacco Heron*, Mallard*, Wood Sandpiper*, Swallow*, House Martin*.
Escapes: Black-rumped Waxbill, Red Avadavat, Yellow-crowned Bishop.
(Passage migrants with an asterisk * have been accepted by the Spanish Rarities Committee, or have been recorded by the author).

Other wildlife:
Rabbit, Canary Lizard (*Gallotia galloti eisentrauti*).

Plain Swift

SECTION 3 (TFNE3)

The sites in this section are good for migrants associated with the pine forest. Las Lagunetas (TFNE3.1) is of particular interest as the tiny, often elusive Canary Islands Kinglet is more accessible here. Blue Chaffinch can be observed at some lookouts (TFNE3.2) although better sites are available. Nevertheless, these lookouts provide some of the most impressive scenery on the island, especially during the winter months.

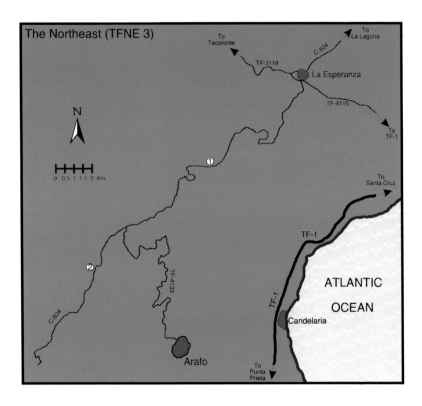

● LAS LAGUNETAS   TFNE3. 1
Category: Protected Scenery

Description:
This is an area of pine forest, which is often swamped in a thick fog. There are a few fields that have been cleared, and which are now used for grazing. These fields are one of the easiest places in Tenerife to observe Canary Islands Kinglet.

Time to visit:
You can visit this site at any time of year, but avoid the bad weather during the winter months.

Canary Islands Kinglet

Location:
From Santa Cruz: Take motorway TF-5 (Autopista del Norte) to the La Laguna and Parque Nacional del Teide exit. Turn left and go past the roundabout, following the signs for La Esperanza (C-824) and Parque Nacional del Teide. 16.1 km after the roundabout, turn right onto a track which leads to Las Lagunetas and park at the bar/restaurant. The bushes on either side of the track are good for the Kinglet.

From Puerto de la Cruz: Take motorway TF-5 (Autopista del Norte) to the La Laguna/ Las Cañadas/Geneto exit (Do not take La Laguna (Por San Benito) Salida 26). At the roundabout turn right towards La Esperanza (C-824) and Parque Nacional del Teide. 16.1 km after the roundabout, turn right onto a track that leads to Las Lagunetas and park at the bar/restaurant. The bushes on either side of the track are good for the Kinglet.

Strategy:
Walk around the fields checking the bushes for Canary Islands Kinglets. The bushes on either side of the road just before you get to the bar/restaurant are also very productive.

Birds:
Year round: Sparrowhawk, Common Buzzard, Common Kestrel, Rock Dove, Plain Swift, Berthelot´s Pipit, Grey Wagtail, Robin, Blackbird, Blackcap, Canary Islands Chiffchaff, Canary Islands Kinglet, Blue Tit, Spanish Sparrow, Chaffinch, Blue Chaffinch, Canary.
Summer visitors: Turtle Dove.
Winter visitors: Song Thrush.
Accidentals: Fieldfare.

● **MIRADOR DE LA CUMBRE**　　　　　　　　　　　　**TFNE3. 2**
Category: Protected Scenery

Description:
This is an interesting lookout where Blue Chaffinch can sometimes be observed. It is worth a visit simply for the spectacular view of Mount Teide and the sea-cloud below.

Time to visit:
All year round.

Location:
From Santa Cruz: Take motorway TF-5 (Autopista del Norte) to the La Laguna and Parque Nacional del Teide exit. Turn left and go through the roundabout, following the sign for La Esperanza (C-824) and Parque Nacional del Teide. 10.1 km from Las Lagunetas, turn right to "Mirador de la Cumbre".

From Puerto de la Cruz: Take motorway TF-5 (Autopista del Norte) to the La Laguna/ Las Cañadas/Geneto exit (Do not take La Laguna (Por San Benito) Salida 26). At the roundabout turn right to La Esperanza (C-824) and Parque Nacional del Teide. 10.1 km from Las Lagunetas, turn right to "Mirador de la Cumbre".

From Las Americas/ Los Cristianos: Take TF-1 and exit at Parque Nacional del Teide. Follow the signs for Vilaflor and Parque Nacional del Teide until you reach the south of the village. Go through Vilaflor and turn right at the crossroads to Parque Nacional del Teide/ La Orotava (C-821). Turn right towards La Laguna (C-824) after about 21.2 km, and then go left to Mirador de la Cumbre.

Strategy:
Wait for Blue Chaffinch to become visible. They sometimes feed on the ground.

Birds:
Year round: Sparrowhawk, Common Kestrel, Rock Dove, Plain Swift, Berthelot´s Pipit, Robin, Canary Islands Chiffchaff, Canary Islands Kinglet, Blue Tit, Blue Chaffinch, Canary.
Summer visitors: Turtle Dove.

Other wildlife:
Reptiles: Canary Lizard.
Butterflies: Red Admiral, Canarian Speckled Wood, Canary Blue.

Blue Tit

TFNE2. 2 LOS RODEOS AIRPORT

TFNE2. 4 VALLE MOLINA RESERVOIR

TFNE2. 5 TEJINA PONDS

TFNE3. 1 LAS LAGUNETAS

TFNE1. 3 ROQUES DE ANAGA

TFNE1. 6 EL BAILADERO

TFNE1. 6 EL BAILADERO & CABEZA DEL TEJO

TFNE1. 8 PICO DEL INGLES

THE
EAST (TFE)

Pallid Swift

THE EAST (TFE)

This is a very dry region of *euphorbia* plants with some scattered cultivated fields. From an ornithological point of view, it is interesting as a small population of the rare Trumpeter Finch still breeds in the area and a breeding colony of Pallid Swift can also be found here during the summer months. The coast is also good for seawatching.

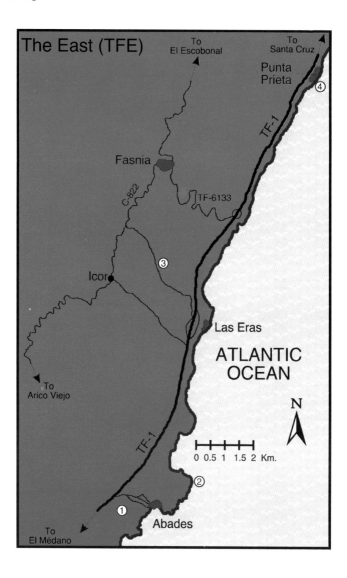

● ABADES

Category: none

Description:
This is an arid area covered with *euphorbia* plants. Trumpeter Finch is sometimes seen drinking from the reservoirs although these are normally dry most of the year. The track is not in very good condition, and a 4WD vehicle is recommended.

Time to visit:
Spring is the best time to visit as the reservoirs are more likely to have some water in it.

Location:
From Santa Cruz: Take motorway TF-1 to Los Cristianos and Aeropuerto del Sur and exit at Abades (Salida 18). Turn right to "La Listada and La Jaca". Turn left or walk onto a dirt track just next to a chalet, about 1.3 km along. You will see the tiny reservoir on the left. There is another reservoir on the same road, a bit to the south. Park anywhere safe.

From Las Americas/ Los Cristianos: Take motorway TF-1 to Santa Cruz and exit at Abades (Salida 18). Turn right to "La Listada and La Jaca". Turn left or walk onto a dirt track just next to a chalet, about 1.3 km along. You will see the tiny reservoir on the left. There is another reservoir on the same road, a bit to the south. Park anywhere safe.

Strategy:
The dirt road is in bad condition, so it is adviseable to walk. Wait for the birds to appear as they visit the reservoir to drink.

Birds:
Year round: Barbary Partridge, Common Kestrel, Little Ringed Plover, Yellow-

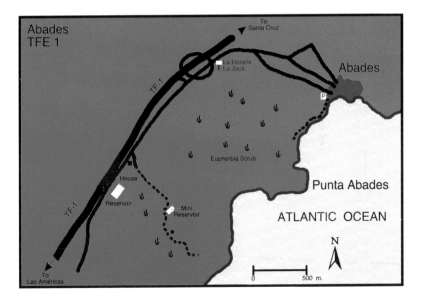

Abades
TFE 1

To Santa Cruz

La Listada
La Jaca

Abades

P

TF-1

Euphorbia Scrub

Punta Abades

House

Reservoir

ATLANTIC OCEAN

Mini Reservoir

TF-1

N

To Las Américas

0   500 m.

legged Gull, Rock Dove, Plain Swift, Berthelot´s Pipit, Spectacled Warbler, Linnet, Trumpeter Finch.
Summer visitors: Turtle Dove, Pallid Swift.
Winter visitors: Cattle Egret, Common Sandpiper.

● PUNTA DE ABONA   TFE2
Category: none

Description:
This is a good seawatching headland, which could be rewarding during migration. Cory´s Shearwater and Little Shearwater have been recorded here, and it is not uncommon to see groups of passing waders during migration.

Time to visit:
The best time is during migration, September to November. The best months for shearwaters are March to November.

Location:
From Santa Cruz: Take motorway TF-1 to Los Cristianos and Aeropuerto del Sur and exit at Poris de Abona (Salida 17). Go through the village and follow the sign for Punta de Abona and La Zarnoza. Park near the lighthouse.

From Las Americas/ Los Cristianos: Take motorway TF-1 to Santa Cruz and exit at Poris de Abona (Salida 17). Go through the village and follow the sign for Punta de Abona and La Zarnoza. Park near the lighthouse.

Strategy:
A telescope is essential for seawatching.

Birds:
Year round: Little Shearwater, Common Kestrel, Yellow-legged Gull, Rock Dove, Plain Swift, Berthelot´s Pipit, Spectacled Warbler, Canary Islands Chiffchaff, Spanish Sparrow.
Summer visitors: Cory´s Shearwater, Turtle Dove, Pallid Swift.
Winter visitors: Ringed Plover, Common Sandpiper.
Passage migrants: Curlew Sandpiper, Whimbrel*.
(Passage migrants with an asterisk * have been recorded by the author).

● LAS ERAS   TFE3
Category: none

Description:
This is an area of *euphorbia* plants with some scattered agricultural fields, which are considered to be one of the most reliable sites for Pallid Swift. Barbary Partridge has also been observed near the cultivated areas.

Time to visit:
The best time to look for Pallid Swift is late May to August although they arrive as early as February.

TF1 ABADES

TF2 PUNTA DE ABONA

TFE3 LAS ERAS

TFE4 PUNTA PRIETA LA CALETA

Location & strategy:
From Santa Cruz: Take motorway TF-1 to Los Cristianos and Aeropuerto del Sur and exit at Las Eras (Salida 16). Go right immediately onto a secondary road and park after 1.6 km in a lay-by on the left. From this spot you can look for Barbary Partridge in the cultivated fields on the opposite side of the road. Carry on up the road up and turn left at the T-junction signposted "Las Eras and La Guera". This is a good area for swifts. Park anywhere safe and beware of fast moving vehicles.

From Las Americas/ Los Cristianos: Take motorway TF-1 to Los Cristianos and Aeropuerto del Sur and exit at Las Eras. Pass the bridge and take the secondary road towards Santa Cruz. After about 1.6 km, park in the lay-by on the left and look for Barbary Partridge in the cultivated fields on the opposite side of the road. Carry on up the road and turn left at the T-junction signposted "Las Eras and La Guera". This area is good for swifts. Park anywhere safe and beware of fast moving vehicles. Plain Swift also occurs in this area, so there are occasional identification problems. Drive around until you see the swifts in flight.

Birds:
Year round: Common Kestrel, Barbary Partridge, Yellow-legged Gull, Rock Dove, Plain Swift, Berthelot´s Pipit, Spectacled Warbler, Spanish Sparrow, Linnet.
Summer visitors: Turtle Dove, Pallid Swift.

● PUNTA PRIETA LA CALETA   TFE4
Category: none

Description:
This is a very small fishing village. Plain Swift and Pallid Swift breed in the cave at the southernmost point, and both species can be observed here together. This site is also good for seawatching during strong winds.

Time to visit:
The best time to look for Pallid Swift is late May to August although they visit the island as early as February.

Pallid Swift

Location:
From Santa Cruz: Take motorway TF-1 to Los Cristianos and Aeropuerto del Sur and exit at Punta Prieta la Caleta (Salida 12), which is 0.7 km after the tunnel. Pass the bridge and turn right at La Caleta, following the road southwards for 2 km until you come to the end. After a steep right- hand bend, park near the houses on your right.

From Las Americas/ Los Cristianos: Take motorway TF-1 to Santa Cruz and exit at Punta Prieta la Caleta (Salida 12), which is 0.7 km before the tunnel. Turn right at La Caleta and follow the road southwards for 2 km until you come to the end. After a steep right-hand bend, park near the houses on your right.

Strategy:
The birds visit this site mainly in late afternoon. Wait for the birds to get into their holes.

Birds:
Year round: Common Kestrel, Yellow-legged Gull, Rock Dove, Plain Swift, Berthelot´s Pipit, Spectacled Warbler, Spanish Sparrow.
Summer visitors: Cory´s Shearwater, Pallid Swift.

Other wildlife:
Bottlenose Dolphin.

Spanish Sparrow

THE CENTRE (TFC)

Blue Chaffinch

THE CENTRE (TFC)

This region encompasses two of Tenerife´s most important ecological zones; the pine forest and the high mountain zone.

The pine forest surrounding Mount Teide is found on the south-facing slopes at altitudes between 800 m (2600 ft) and 2200 m (7200 ft). The endemic Canary Pine is resistant to fire, so it can produce new shoots after having been burnt. The pine forest is home to Blue Chaffinch, and you can see it quite easily at several sites; (TFC2, TFC3, TFC4, TFC7, TFC8).

The High Mountain Zone starts at about 2000 m (6500 ft) and is very well represented in the Teide National Park (TFC5, TFC6). Only a few species of bird breed here, but the jagged mountains with their spectacular lava formations and the dramatic landscape, dominated by "Father Teide", are well worth visiting. In winter the highest areas are usually covered with snow.

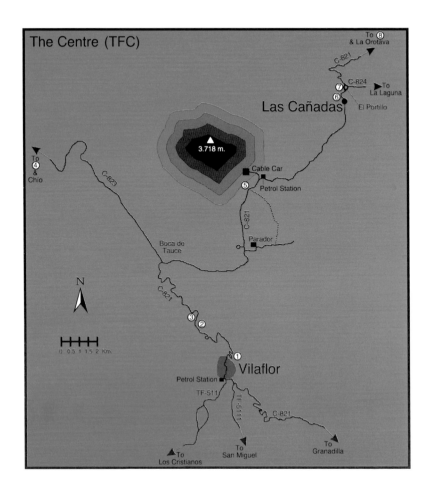

● VILAFLOR   TFC1
Category: none

Description:
This is the highest village in Tenerife and is located at the beginning of the pine forest where a good number of endemics can be found.

Time to visit:
You can visit this site at any time of the year although May to July is the best period for catching Blue Chaffinch in song.

Location:
From Santa Cruz: Take motorway TF-1 to Los Cristianos and exit at Granadilla/El Medano (Salida 22). Follow the signs to Granadilla (TF-614), and once in the town, turn left after passing the two petrol stations on your left. Turn right immediately onto C-821 to Vilaflor, which is not signposted. Follow the signs for Vilaflor and Parque Nacional del Teide. Once you reach Vilaflor and the T-junction, park near the bar/restaurant to check the fields and wires south of the village. Carry on for a further 2 km to reach "Pino Gordo" and park in the car park.

From Puerto de la Cruz: Take TF-5 to La Orotava and follow the signs for Parque Nacional del Teide (C-821). Cross the National Park and turn left at Boca de Tauce towards Vilaflor (C-821). After 14 km, you will get to "Pino Gordo", and you can park in the car park. Carry on for a further 2 km to get to the south of the village. After the petrol station on your right, you will see a bar/restaurant. Park just near here to check the fields and wires to the south.

From Las Americas/ Los Cristianos: Take TF-1 and exit at Parque Nacional del Teide. Follow the signs for Vilaflor and Parque Nacional del Teide until you reach the south of the village. Park near the bar/restaurant to check the fields and wires to the south.
After another 2 km, turn right at the "Pino Gordo" car park.

Strategy:
The fields to the south of Vilaflor are good for finches. Check the electric wires for Rock Sparrow. About 2 km to the north, there is a large pine tree, known as "Pino Gordo", which attracts a good variety of endemic bird species and subspecies. You can park in the car park.

Birds:
Year round: Sparrowhawk, Common Kestrel, Barbary Partridge, Rock Dove, Long-eared Owl, Plain Swift, Great Spotted Woodpecker, Berthelot´s Pipit, Grey Wagtail, Spectacled Warbler, Sardinian Warbler, Blackcap, Canary Islands Chiffchaff, Canary Islands Kinglet, Blue Tit, Raven, Blue Chaffinch, Canary, Corn Bunting.
Summer visitors: Turtle Dove, Pallid Swift.

● THE LEAKING PIPE   TFC2
Category: Natural Park

Description:
Interesting birds are attracted to this area to drink, and it can sometimes be an excellent site for photography.

Time to visit:
You can visit all year round although summer months are best, and especially around midday, when the temperatures are at their highest.

Location:
From Santa Cruz: Take motorway TF-1 to Los Cristianos and exit at Granadilla/El Medano (Salida 22). Follow the signs to Granadilla (TF-614) and once in the town, turn left after passing the two petrol stations on your left. Turn right immediately onto C-821 to Vilaflor, which is not signposted. Follow the signs for Vilaflor and Parque Nacional del Teide. This site is 9.6 km from the petrol station at Vilaflor. Look for the signs "Respetemos la Naturaleza" and "Peligro de Incendio" on your right. Park near these signs and cross to the opposite side of the road to reach the pipe.

From Puerto de la Cruz: Take TF-5 to La Orotava and follow the signs to Parque Nacional del Teide (C-821). Cross the National Park and turn left at the crossroads (Boca de Tauce) to Vilaflor (C-821). After 6.4 km, park on the left near the signs "Respetemos la Naturaleza" and "Peligro de Incendio". Cross to the opposite side of the road to reach the pipe.

From Las Americas/ Los Cristianos: Take TF-1 and exit at Parque Nacional del Teide. Follow the signs to Vilaflor and Parque Nacional del Teide until you reach the south of the village. This site is 9.6 km from the petrol station at Vilaflor. Look for the signs "Respetemos la Naturaleza" and "Peligro de Incendio" on your right. Park near these signs and cross to the opposite side of the road to reach the pipe.

Strategy:
Wait for the birds to come and drink.

Birds:
Year round: Sparrowhawk, Common Kestrel, Rock Dove, Plain Swift, Great Spotted Woodpecker, Berthelot´s Pipit, Grey Wagtail, Blackcap, Canary Islands Chiffchaff, Canary Islands Kinglet, Blue Tit, Raven, Blue Chaffinch, Canary.
Summer visitors: Turtle Dove, Pallid Swift.

● **LAS LAJAS**   **TFC3**
Category: Natural Park

Description:
This picnic area in the pine forest is considered to be the best place in the Western Palearctic to see the endemic Blue Chaffinch, and surprisingly, these birds are often quite tame and approachable. There is also a fairly good population of Great Spotted Woodpecker breeding at this site.

Time to visit:
This is a good site to visit all year round.

Location:
From Santa Cruz: Take motorway TF-1 to Los Cristianos and exit at Granadilla/El Medano (Salida 22). Follow the signs to Granadilla (TF-614), and once in the town, turn left after passing the two petrol stations on your left. Turn right immediately onto C-821 to Vilaflor, which is not signposted. Follow the signs for

Blue Chaffinch

Vilaflor and Parque Nacional del Teide. This picnic area is 10.8 km from the petrol station at Vilaflor. Turn left at the sign for "Las Lajas".

From Puerto de la Cruz: Take TF-5 to La Orotava and follow the signs to Parque Nacional del Teide (C-821). Cross the National Park and turn left at the crossroads (Boca de Tauce) to Vilaflor (C-821). 5.2 km from the crossroads (Boca de Tauce), turn left to "Las Lajas".

From Las Americas/ Los Cristianos: Take TF-1 and exit at Parque Nacional del Teide. Follow the signs for Vilaflor and Parque Nacional del Teide until you get to the south of the village. The picnic area is 10.8 km from the petrol station at Vilaflor. Turn left at the sign for "Las Lajas".

Strategy:
Walk round the tables looking for chaffinches, which are often feeding on the ground or singing in the pines. Common Chaffinch has not colonised this habitat, so all the chaffinches you see here will be Blue Chaffinch. The woodpecker can be seen pecking away at the pines, and it is most commonly detected by its "chick" call.

Birds:
Year round: Sparrowhawk, Common Kestrel, Rock Dove, Plain Swift, Great Spotted Woodpecker, Berthelot´s Pipit, Canary Islands Chiffchaff, Canary Islands Kinglet, Blue Tit, Raven, Blue Chaffinch, Canary.
Summer visitors: Turtle Dove, Pallid Swift.

● ZONA RECREATIVA CHIO   TFC4
Category: Natural Park

Description:
Blue Chaffinch can be expected at this site, but Great Spotted Woodpecker is scarce.

Time to visit:
It is possible to visit this site all year round.

Location:
From Santa Cruz: Take motorway TF-1 to Los Cristianos and exit at Granadilla/El

Médano (Salida 22). Follow the signs to Granadilla (TF-614), and once in the town, turn left after passing the two petrol stations on your left. Turn right immediately onto C-821 to Vilaflor, which is not signposted. Follow the signs for Vilaflor and Parque Nacional del Teide. Go through Vilaflor and turn left at the crossroads (Boca de Tauce) to Guia de Isora (C-823). 12.5 km from the crossroads (Boca de Tauce), turn left into the picnic area signposted "Zona Recreativa Chio".

From Puerto de la Cruz: Take TF-5 to La Orotava and follow the signs for Parque Nacional del Teide (C-821). Cross the National Park and continue on to Guia de Isora (C-823). 12.5 km from the crossroads (Boca de Tauce), turn left into the picnic area, which will be signposted "Zona Recreativa Chio".

From Las Americas/ Los Cristianos: Take TF-1 and exit at Parque Nacional del Teide. Follow the sings to Vilaflor and Parque Nacional del Teide until you reach the south of the village. Go through Vilaflor and turn left at the crossroads (Boca de Tauce) to Guia de Isora (C-823). 12.5 km from the crossroads, turn left into the picnic area, which will be signposted "Zona Recreativa Chio".

Strategy:
Walk round the picnic area looking for birds.

Birds:
Year round: Sparrowhawk, Common Kestrel, Rock Dove, Plain Swift, Great Spotted Woodpecker, Berthelot´s Pipit, Canary Islands Chiffchaff, Canary Islands Kinglet, Blue Tit, Raven, Blue Chaffinch, Canary.
Summer visitors: Turtle Dove, Pallid Swift.

● **SIETE CAÑADAS**   **TFC5**
Category: National Park

Description:
This is actually a very pleasant walk through the upper section of Teide National Park. The speciality here is Southern Grey Shrike, which can be found with a little patience. Berthelot´s Pipit and Canary are common and easier to see.

Time to visit:
It is possible to visit all year round although during the winter months there is often snow and the park is sometimes closed to the public.

Location:
From Santa Cruz: Take motorway TF-1 to Los Cristianos and exit at Granadilla/El Medano (Salida 22). Follow the signs for Granadilla (TF-614) and once in the town, turn left after passing the two petrol stations on your left. Turn right immediately onto C-821 to Vilaflor, which is not signposted. Follow the signs for Vilaflor and Parque Nacional del Teide. Go through Vilaflor and turn right at the crossroads marked Parque Nacional del Teide/ La Orotava (C-821). 10.2 km after the crossroads (Boca de Tauce), park in the lay-by on your right. Look for the sign "Base del Teide 2250 m".

From Puerto de la Cruz: Take TF-5 to La Orotava and follow the signs to Parque Nacional del Teide (C-821). Enter the National Park and about 11 km from the Information Centre, park in the lay-by on your left. Look for the sign "Base del Teide 2250 m".

From Las Americas/ Los Cristianos: Take TF-1 and exit at Parque Nacional del Teide. Follow the signs for Vilaflor and Parque Nacional del Teide until you reach the south of the village. Go through Vilaflor and turn right at the crossroads marked Parque Nacional del Teide/ La Orotava (C-821). 10.2 km from the crossroads (Boca de Tauce), park in the lay-by on your right. Look for the sign "Base del Teide 2250 m".

Strategy:
The shrike is best detected from its call. There are not many birds in this area, so check every single one that you see or hear.

Birds:
Year round: Common Kestrel, Rock Dove, Plain Swift, Berthelot´s Pipit, Canary Islands Chiffchaff, Southern Grey Shrike, Canary.

● LAS CAÑADAS INFORMATION CENTRE   TFC6
Category: National Park

Description:
There is a pleasant garden where you can walk round and observe the Canary, which is very common here.

Time to visit:
You can visit all year round although during the winter months there is often snow and the park is sometimes closed to the public.

Location:
From Santa Cruz: Take motorway TF-5 (Autopista del Norte) to the La Laguna and Parque Nacional del Teide exit. Turn left and pass the roundabout, following the sign for La Esperanza (C-824) and Parque Nacional del Teide. Stay on this road until you reach the National Park and then turn left at the T-junction onto C-821. The information centre is on your right and you can park in the car park.

From Puerto de la Cruz: Take TF-5 to La Orotava and follow the signs to Parque Nacional del Teide (C-821). Once in the National Park, follow the road until you see the information centre on your right. Park in the car park.

From Las Americas/ Los Cristianos: Take TF-1 and exit at Parque Nacional del Teide. Follow the signs for Vilaflor and Parque Nacional del Teide until you get to the south of the village. Go through Vilaflor and turn right at the crossroads to Parque Nacional del Teide/ La Orotava (C-821). 21.2 km from the crossroads (Boca de Tauce), turn left into the centre car park.

Strategy:
Walk round the information centre garden to look for birds.

Birds:
Year round: Common Kestrel, Rock Dove, Plain Swift, Berthelot´s Pipit, Canary Islands Chiffchaff, Blue Tit, Canary.

Other wildlife:
Canary Lizard.

● EL PORTILLO   TFC7
Category: National Park

Description:
This is another site for Blue Chaffinch.

Time to visit:
It is possible to visit all year round although during the winter months there is often snow and the park is sometimes closed to the public.

Location:
From Santa Cruz: Take motorway TF-5 (Autopista del Norte) to the La Laguna and Parque Nacional del Teide exit. Turn left and go over the roundabout, following the sign for La Esperanza (C-824) and Parque Nacional del Teide. Follow this road until you reach the T-junction. Park near the bar/restaurant.

From Puerto de la Cruz: Take TF-5 to La Orotava and follow the signs for Parque Nacional del Teide (C-821). Once in the National Park, park near the bar/restaurant at El Portillo.

From Las Americas/ Los Cristianos: Take TF-1 and exit at Parque Nacional del Teide. Follow the signs for Vilaflor and Parque Nacional del Teide until you reach the south of the village. Go through Vilaflor and turn right at the crossroads to Parque Nacional del Teide/ La Orotava (C-821). 21.5 km after the crossroads (Boca de Tauce), park near the bar/restaurant at El Portillo.

Strategy:
Look for birds in the trees near the bar/restaurant.

Birds:
Year round: Common Kestrel, Rock Dove, Plain Swift, Berthelot´s Pipit, Canary Islands Chiffchaff, Robin, Blue Tit, Blue Chaffinch, Canary.

Other wildlife:
Canary Lizard.

● GALERIA PINO DE LA CRUZ   TFC8
Category: Natural Park

Description:
This is another picnic area where you can find Blue Chaffinch.

Time to visit:
You can visit this site all year round, but it is best to avoid the winter months.

Location:
From Santa Cruz: Take motorway TF-5 (Autopista del Norte) to the La Laguna and Parque Nacional del Teide exit. Turn left and go over the roundabout, following the sign for La Esperanza (C-824) and Parque Nacional del Teide. Stay on this road until you reach the T-junction at the National Park. Turn right towards La Orotava (C-821). Park at the small picnic area on your right after about 7.5 km.

<u>From Puerto de la Cruz:</u> Take TF-5 to La Orotava and follow the signs for Parque Nacional del Teide (C-821). 7.5 km before you get to the National Park and the T-junction at El Portillo, turn left into a small picnic area signposted "Galeria Pino de la Cruz".

<u>From Las Americas/ Los Cristianos:</u> Take TF-1 and exit at Parque Nacional del Teide. Follow the signs for Vilaflor and Parque Nacional del Teide until you reach the south of the village. Go through Vilaflor and turn right at the crossroads (Boca de Tauce) to Parque Nacional del Teide/ La Orotava (C-821). After 21.2 km you come to another crossroads where you carry on in the direction of La Orotava. After about 7.5 km, you will see the picnic area sign-posted "Galeria Pino de la Cruz" on your right.

Strategy:
Walk round the picnic tables looking for birds.

Birds:
<u>Year round:</u> Common Kestrel, Rock Dove, Plain Swift, Canary Islands Chiffchaff, Blue Tit, Blue Chaffich, Canary.

Canary Islands Chiffchaff

Great Spotted Woodpecker

TFC3 LAS LAJAS

TFC5 SIETE CAÑADAS

TFC1 VILAFLOR (PINO GORDO)

SELECTED BIRD SPECIES

Bulwer´s Petrel *(Bulweria bulwerii):*
This species can arrive as early as February, but visits the colonies in mid-April or early May when it is easy to observe. It leaves again in September. This breeding summer visitor is best seen from the ferry to Gomera (TFS3) although it can sometimes be recorded from the ferry to Gran Canaria (TFNE1.2) and between Tenerife and the Salvages (TFNE1.4).

Cory´s Shearwater *(Calonectris diomedea borealis):*
This is a summer visitor, most commonly seen between the months of February and November. Good views can be obtained during the ferry-crossings to Gomera (TFS3) and Gran Canaria (TFNE1.2), and on the boat trip to Roques de Anaga (TFNE1.3) and the Salvages (TFNE1.4). It can also be seen from the coast at various sites: (TFS7), (TFS8), (TFS9), (TFS14), (TFNW6), (TFNW7), (TFNW8), (TFN1), (TFNE1.5), (TFNE1.7), (TFNE2.6), (TFE1), (TFE2), (TFE4).

Manx Shearwater *(Puffinus puffinus):*
This bird arrives in the Archipelago in February and departs in June although passage migrants can be observed during autumn migration and especially in September. As with Little Shearwater, the best way to see this species is during the ferry crossings to Gran Canaria (TFNE12) and to Gomera (TFS3). There is a very small population on Tenerife that breeds in the laurel forest.

Little Shearwater *(Puffinus assimilis baroli):*
Resident in the Canary Islands, it is best observed from the ferries to Gomera (TFS3) and Gran Canaria (TFNE1.2), as well as during the boat trips to Roques de Anaga (TFNE1.3) and the Salvages (TFNE1.4). It can sometimes be seen from different headlands: (TFS7), (TFS8), (TFNW6), (TFNW8), (TFE2). Breeding from March to June, it is more frequently observed during the summer and autumn months.

White-faced Storm-petrel *(Pelagodroma marina hypoleuca):*
A rare breeding bird which visits the Eastern Canaries from February to June. Very easy to observe around the Salvage Islands (TFNE1.4).

European Storm-petrel *(Hydrobates pelagicus):*
A scarce summer breeder arriving at the colonies between June and October although it can be recorded from mid-May onwards. The best way to observe it is from the ferry to Gomera (TFS3) or at Roques de Anaga (TFNE1.3).

Madeiran Storm-petrel *(Oceanodroma castro):*
This localised winter visitor breeds on the remote islets of Roques de Anaga (TFNE1.3), which can be reached by chartering a boat from Santa Cruz. It is present from the end of September to mid February. Mid-October is a good month to try to see it.

Osprey *(Pandion haliaetus):*
This uncommon resident can sometimes be seen fishing on man-made reservoirs. Migratory individuals have also been recorded: (TFS7), (TFSW4), (TFNW6), (TFN6).

Barbary Falcon *(Falco pelegrinoides):*
A scarce, localised resident that you can bank on seeing around their breeding grounds (TFNW6). Courtship starts in February, and juveniles are seen hunting in the summer months. It has been recorded at: (TFS7), (TFS11), (TFNW7), (TFNE1.1), (TFNE1.6), (TFNE1.7), (TFNE1.8), (TFNE2.5).

Barbary Partridge *(Alectoris barbara koenigi):*
This species can turn up in many different sites. The population fluctuates from year to year, depending on the hunting. The most reliable sites for observing it are (TFSW1) and (TFC1) although it can sometimes be seen at (TFS5), (TFNW4), (TFNW6), (TFE1), and (TFE3).

Quail *(Coturnix coturnix):*
This elusive bird species is more often heard than seen. Interesting sites to look for it include; (TFNE2.2), (TFNE2.3), (TFNE2.4).

Stone-curlew *(Burhinus oedicnemus distinctus):*
This scarce localised species favours arid semi-desert steppes and can only be found in the south of the island. It is more often heard than seen.
Sites: (TFS4), (TFS7), (TFS10), (TFS11), (TFS12), (TFSW4).

Kentish Plover *(Charadrius alexandrinus):*
Best seen at the last breeding site in Tenerife (TFS14). Some migratory birds congregate at this site in winter.

Woodcock *(Scolopax rusticola):*
This elusive bird species associated with the laurel forest and occasionally the banana plantations is extremely difficult to find. Several sites to look for it are: (TFSW5), (TFNW3), (TFN3).

Common Tern *(Sterna hirundo)*:
This localised species breeds sporadically on Tenerife during the summer. Passing birds can also be seen. Sites to look for it include: (TFS3), (TFS14), (TFNE1.2), (TFNE1.3), (TFNE1.4), (TFNE1.5).

Bolle´s Pigeon *(Columba bollii)*:
Associated with the dense laurel forest in the mountainous areas, this endemic bird species is not so difficult to detect in flight. It breeds from January to September, becoming more visible after incubation around mid-March. Several reliable sites include: (TFNW3), (TFN3), (TFNE1.6), (TFNE1.8). Perched views can sometimes be obtained with patience.

Laurel Pigeon *(Columba junoniae)*:
This beautiful pigeon, which is becoming one of the most difficult endemic bird species to see on Tenerife, is associated with the "Thermophylic woods", but is mainly recorded in the laurel forest and nearby cultivated fields. It is sometimes seen travelling to private cultivated areas (TFN5), where it feeds on various fruit trees. It is usually recorded from March to September, and the most reliable site to look for this scarce endemic is Ladera de Tigaiga (TFN3) although it can be seen with patience at Monte del Agua (TFNW3). During the summer months, in particular August, and in late January/early February, it can sometimes be seen at Pico del Ingles (TFNE1.8) where it is considered rare. Perched views of this species are very hard to get on Tenerife, but easier on other islands (Gomera and La Palma).

Barn Owl (*Tyto alba*):
The rarest breeding owl on Tenerife, but still fairly common in some areas. One of the most reliable sites to look for it is Los Rodeos Airport (TFNE 2.2).

Long-eared Owl (*Asio otus canariensis*):
Although it can be seen throughout the island, the most reliable site is Los Rodeos Airport (TFNE2.2).

Plain Swift (*Apus unicolor*):
This Macaronesian endemic is the commonest swift on Tenerife and can easily be found around the island at many different sites. It is the only endemic known to winter outside the Archipelago. Part of the population migrates to North Africa at the end of September until the end of December/January. Beware of Pallid Swift that arrives on the Island in February and departs in October.

Pallid Swift (*Apus pallidus brehmorum*):
This species is more difficult to find as it is very unpredictable. It can easily be seen near its breeding colonies. Two of the most reliable sites are Punta Prieta la Caleta (TFE4) and Las Eras (TFE3).
Other sites where it has been recorded include: (TFS4), (TFS7), (TFS11), (TFSW4), (TFNW3), (TFN4), (TFNE1.8), (TFNE2.4), (TFNE2.5), (TFNE2.6).

Hoopoe (*Upupa epops pulchra*):
It is not hard to find this butterfly-like bird on Tenerife if you look in the right place. It is becoming increasingly associated with the golf courses in the south of the island, where it searches for insects in the green grass. Some of the most reliable sites include; Ten-Bel (TFS9), Amarilla Golf (TFS11), Golf del Sur (TFS12).

Great Spotted Woodpecker (*Dendrocopos major canariensis*):
Associated with the pine forest, this endemic resident subspecies is very accessible and tame at the "Las Lajas" picnic site near Vilaflor (TFC3). It can also be found around Vilaflor itself (TFC1).

Lesser Short-toed Lark (*Calandrella rufescens rufescens*):
This rare subspecies is now an endangered species and is only found in cultivated fields or grasslands. The only reliable site is Los Rodeos Airport (TFNE2.2).

Lesser Short-toed Lark (*Calandrella rufescens polatzeki*):
Found only in the arid semi-desert steppe in the south of the island, this species is becoming very rare and can only be looked for with some degree of success at Guargacho (TFS10) and/or Amarilla Golf (TFS11).

Berthelot´s Pipit (*Anthus berthelotii berthelotii*):
This is an abundant Macaronesian endemic, which can be found anywhere between sea level and the peak of Mount Teide.

Spectacled Warbler (*Sylvia conspicillata orbitalis*):
Occurs mainly in the lower zone of Tenerife and can be relatively easy to find, especially in the south of the island.

Sardinian Warbler (*Sylvia melanocephala leucogastra*):
This bird lives in cultivated and well-vegetated areas. It is not uncommon in the North of Tenerife.

Canary Islands Chiffchaff (*Phylloscopus canariensis*):
This is the most abundant endemic bird species on Tenerife. Found in all habitats and ecological zones.

Canary Islands Kinglet (*Regulus teneriffae*):
Despite being resident in several different forests on the island, it is easier to observe in the laurel forest and near Las Lagunetas (TFNE3.1).

Blue Tit (*Parus caeruleus teneriffae*):
This is a very common endemic bird subspecies which is quite different from the continental race. Its endemic status will probably change in the near future. It occurs mainly in the forests in Tenerife although it might move to lower altitudes in the winter.

Southern Grey Shrike (*Lanius meridionalis koenigi*):
This species is fairly common in the lower zone at (TFS4), (TFS6), (TFS7), (TFS10), (TFS11), (TFS12), (TFS14), and less common at Siete Cañadas (TFC5) in the National Park.

Spanish Sparrow (*Passer hispaniolensis*):
This is the most abundant sparrow on Tenerife.

Rock Sparrow (*Petronia petronia madeirensis*):
A very scarce, localised sparrow that can best be observed at their breeding site at Teno Alto (TFNW5) and in great numbers at the lower zone of Teno Natural Park (TFNW6) where they concentrate to overwinter from December until February.

Chaffinch (*Fringilla coelebs tintillon*):
A fairly common endemic bird subspecies in the north of the island. Sites to look for it include; (TFNW3), (TFN3), (TFNE1.6), (TFNE1.8), (TFNE3.1).

Blue Chaffinch (*Fringilla teydea teydea*):
This emblematic endemic bird species is confined to Tenerife and Gran Canaria and can be found nowhere else in the world. Associated only with the pine forest, where the Common Chaffinch does not occur, the Blue Chaffinch can reliably be found at the "Las Lajas" picnic site near Vilaflor (TFC3), and can also be seen at: (TFN2), (TFC2), (TFC4), (TFC7), (TFC8), (TFNE3.1), (TFNE3.2).

Serin (*Serinus serinus*):
Almost identical to the Canary, but localised on Tenerife, where it can be found at La Laguna (TFNE2.1) and El Peñon Golfcourse (TFNE2.3) and occasionally at Valle Molina Reservoir (TFNE2.4).

Canary (*Serinus canaria*):
This is an abundant Macaronesian endemic, found in a wide range of habitats from sea-level up as far as the mountain zone. It does not show a predilection for the southern arid part of the island.

Trumpeter Finch (*Bucanetes githagineus amantum*):
This species has drastically declined on Tenerife in the last decade and is now confined to a few areas in the south of the island. It can sometimes be observed at: (TFS4), (TFS7), (TFS14), (TFE1).

FULL SPECIES CHECKLIST

This checklist has been compiled using information from three main sources: "Catálogo y Biliografía de la Avifauna Canaria" (1976-1994) by Keith Emmerson *et. al.* (although only 22% of this dubious data is included), the official records reported in "Ardeola" (SEO/Birdlife) between 1984 and 1998, and records from my own experiences in the field.

Ship assisted species and escapes have not been included, and the Spanish Rarities Committee (Comité de Rarezas de la SEO) has not yet accepted a few species on the list.

I would like to encourage all visitors, whether beginner or keen birder, to submit their records to the official Spanish Rarities Committee and the author at:

SEO/Birdlife
Comité de Rarezas
C/ Melquiades Biencinto 34
E-28053
Madrid
Spain

Eduardo García del Rey
C/ Fdo Barajas Vilchez 9
38004 Santa Cruz de Tenerife
Canary Islands
Spain

If you have found a rare bird and would like to report it, please call the **CANARY ISLANDS BIRDLINE** at: 00 34 922 27 99 58 (from the UK) or 922 27 99 58 (from Tenerife).

Key to the status:

R= Resident
S= Summer visitor
W= Winter visitor
WB= Winter breeder
P= Passage migrant
A= Accidental
I= Introduced
E= Extinct

1= Abundant
2= Common
3= Fairly common or widespread
4= Uncommon, scarce or localised
5= Rare or very localised

Endemic status:
CIE= Canary Islands endemic
ME= Macaronesian endemic
SCCI= Subspecies confined to Canary Island
SCM= Subspecies confined to Macaronesia

STATUS	SPECIES	SCIENTIFIC NAME	Endemic							
A	Pied-billed Grebe	Podilymbus podiceps								
A	Little Grebe	Tachybaptus ruficollis								
P4/W5	Black-necked Grebe	Podiceps nigricollis								
A	Fea´s/Zinos Petrel	Pterodroma feae/madeira								
S4	Bulwer´s Petrel	Bulweria bulwerii								
S1	Cory´s Shearwater	Calonectris diomedea borealis	SCM							
P4	Great Shearwater	Puffinus gravis								
A	Sooty Shearwater	Puffinus griseus								

STATUS	SPECIES	SCIENTIFIC NAME	Endemic										
S5/P4	Manx Shearwater	Puffinus puffinus											
R4	Little Shearwater	Puffinus assimilis baroli	SCM										
A	Wilson´s Storm-petrel	Oceanites oceanicus											
A	White-faced Storm-petrel	Pelagodroma marina											
S4	European Storm-petrel	Hydrobates pelagicus											
A	Leach´s Storm-petrel	Oceanodroma leucorhoa											
WB4	Madeiran Storm-petrel	Oceanodroma castro											
A	Red-billed Tropicbird	Phaethon aethereus											
P4/W4	Gannet	Morus bassanus											
P5	Cormorant	Phalacrocorax carbo											
A	Bittern	Botaurus stellaris											
A	American Bittern	Botaurus lentiginosus											
P4/S5	Little Bittern	Ixobrychus minutus											
A	Dwarf Bittern	Ixobrychus stumii											
P4	Night Heron	Nycticorax nycticorax											
P5	Squacco Heron	Ardeola ralloides											
P4/W4	Cattle Egret	Bubulcus ibis											
A	Western Reef Egret	Egretta gularis											
R3	Little Egret	Egretta garzetta											
A	Great White Egret	Egretta alba											
R3	Grey Heron	Ardea cinerea											
A	Great Blue Heron	Ardea herodias											
P4	Purple Heron	Ardea purpurea											
A	Black Stork	Ciconia nigra											
P5/W5	White Stork	Ciconia ciconia											
A	Glossy Ibis	Plegadis falcinellus											
P4/W4	Spoonbill	Platalea leucorodia											
A	Greater Flamingo	Phoenicopterus ruber											
A	White-faced Whistling Duck	Dendrocygna viduata											
A	White-fronted Goose	Anser albifrons											
A	Greylag Goose	Anser anser											
A	Brent Goose	Branta bernicla											
A	Shelduck	Tadorna tadorna											
W4	Wigeon	Anas penelope											
A	American Wigeon	Anas americana											
W4	Gadwall	Anas strepera											
W3	Common Teal	Anas crecca crecca											
A	Green-winged Teal	Anas crecca carolinensis											
W4	Mallard	Anas platyrhynchos											
A	Black Duck	Anas rubripes											
W4	Pintail	Anas acuta											
P4/W4	Garganey	Anas querquedula											
A	Blue-winged Teal	Anas discors											

STATUS	SPECIES	SCIENTIFIC NAME	Endemic
P4/W4	Shoveler	Anas clypeata	
A	Marbled Duck	Marmaronetta angustirostris	
A	Red-crested Pochard	Netta rufina	
W4	Pochard	Aythya ferina	
A	Ring-necked Duck	Aythya collaris	
P4/W4	Tufted Duck	Aythya fuligula	
A	Scaup	Aythya marila	
A	Lesser Scaup	Aythya affinis	
A	Red-breasted Merganser	Mergus serrator	
A	Honey Buzzard	Pernis apivorus	
P4	Black Kite	Milvus migrans	
E	Red Kite	Milvus milvus	
A	White-tailed Eagle	Haliaeetus albicilla	
E	Egyptian Vulture	Neophron pernopterus	
P5	Short-toed Eagle	Circaetus gallicus	
P4/W5	Marsh Harrier	Circus aeruginosus	
P4/W5	Hen Harrier	Circus cyaneus	
A	Pallid Harrier	Circus macrourus	
P4	Montagu´s Harrier	Circus pygargus	
R3	Sparrowhawk	Accipiter nisus granti	SCM
R3	Common Buzzard	Buteo buteo insularum	SCCI
A	Golden Eagle	Aquila chrysaetos	
P5	Booted Eagle	Hieraaetus pennatus	
A	Bonelli´s Eagle	Hieraetus fasciatus	
R4/P4	Osprey	Pandion haliaetus	
A	Lesser Kestrel	Falco naumanni	
R1	Common Kestrel	Falco tinnunculus canariensis	SCM
A	Red-footed Falcon	Falco vespertinus	
A	Merlin	Falco columbarius	
P4	Hobby	Falco subbuteo	
A	Eleonora´s Falcon	Falco eleonorae	
A	Lanner Falcon	Falco biarmicus	
P4/W4	Peregrine Falcon	Falco peregrinus	
R4	Barbary Falcon	Falco pelegrinoides	
R3	Barbary Partridge	Alectoris barbara koenigi	
R3/P4	Quail	Coturnix coturnix	
P4	Spotted Crake	Porzana porzana	
P5	Little Crake	Porzana parva	
P5	Baillon´s Crake	Porzana pusilla	
A	Corn Crake	Crex crex	
R3	Moorhen	Gallinula chloropus	
A	Allen´s Gallinule	Porphyrula alleni	
A	American Purple Gallinule	Porphyrula martinica	

135

STATUS	SPECIES	SCIENTIFIC NAME	Endemic								
R4/W3	Coot	Fulica atra									
A	Red-knobbed Coot	Fulica cristata									
A	Little Bustard	Tetrax tetrax									
P4/W5	Oystercatcher	Haematopus ostralegus									
P4	Black-winged Stilt	Himantopus himantopus									
P4	Avocet	Recurvirostra avosetta									
R4	Stone-curlew	Burhinus oedicnemus distinctus	SCCI								
P4	Cream-coloured Courser	Cursorius cursor bannermani	SCCI								
P4	Collared Pratincole	Glareola pranticola									
R3	Little Ringed Plover	Charadrius dubius									
P3/W3	Ringed Plover	Charadrius hiaticula									
R4/W4	Kentish Plover	Charadrius alexandrinus									
P5/W5	Dotterel	Charadrius morinellus									
A	American Golden Plover	Pluvialis dominica									
P5/W4	European Golden Plover	Pluvialis apricaria									
P4/W2	Grey Plover	Pluvialis squatarola									
A	White-tailed Lapwing	Vanellus leucurus									
P3/W4	Lapwing	Vanellus vanellus									
P4/W5	Knot	Calidris canutus									
W4	Sanderling	Calidris alba									
A	Western Sandpiper	Calidris mauri									
P4/W4	Little Stint	Calidris minuta									
P5	Temminck´s Stint	Calidris temminckii									
A	White-rumped Sandpiper	Calidris fuscicollis									
A	Baird´s Sandpiper	Calidris bairdii									
A	Pectoral Sandpiper	Calidris melanotos									
P4	Curlew Sandpiper	Calidris ferruginea									
A	Purple Sandpiper	Calidris maritima									
P3/W4	Dunlin	Calidris alpina									
A	Buff-breasted Sandpiper	Tryngites subruficollis									
P4	Ruff	Philomachus pugnax									
P5/W5	Jack Snipe	Lymnocryptes minimus									
P3/W2	Common Snipe	Gallinago gallinago									
A	Great Snipe	Gallinago media									
A	Long-billed Dowitcher	Limnodromus scolopaceus									
R4	Woodcock	Scolopax rusticola									
P4/W4	Black-tailed Godwit	Limosa limosa									
P4/W4	Bar-tailed Godwit	Limosa lapponica									
P3/W2	Whimbrel	Numenius phaeopus									
P4/W4	Curlew	Numenius arquata									
P4/W5	Spotted Redshank	Tringa erytropus									
P3/W4	Common Redshank	Tringa totanus									
A	Marsh Sandpiper	Tringa stagnatilis									
P4/W3	Greenshank	Tringa nebularia									

STATUS	SPECIES	SCIENTIFIC NAME	Endemic								
A	Lesser Yellowlegs	Tringa flavipes									
P4/W4	Green Sandpiper	Tringa ochropus									
P3/W5	Wood Sandpiper	Tringa glareola									
P3/W2	Common Sandpiper	Actitis hypoleucos									
A	Spotted Sandpiper	Actitis macularia									
P3/W2	Turnstone	Arenaria interpres									
P4/W5	Grey Phalarope	Phalaropus fulicaria									
P4	Pomarine Skua	Stercorarius pomarinus									
P5	Arctic Skua	Stercorarius parasiticus									
P5	Long-tailed Skua	Stercorarius longicaudus									
P4/W5	Great Skua	Stercorarius skua									
W5	Mediterranean Gull	Larus melanocephalus									
A	Little Gull	Larus minutus									
A	Sabine´s Gull	Larus sabini									
P3/W2	Black-headed Gull	Larus ridibundus									
P5/W4	Audouin´s Gull	Larus audouinii									
A	Ring-billed Gull	Larus delawarensis									
A	Common Gull	Larus canus									
P4/W3	Lesser Black-backed Gull	Larus fuscus									
A	Herring Gull	Larus argentatus									
R1	Yellow-legged Gull	Larus cachinnans atlantis	SCM								
A	Great Black-backed Gull	Larus marinus									
P5/W4	Kittiwake	Rissa tridactyla									
A	Gull-billed Tern	Gelochelidon nilotica									
P3/W2	Sandwich Tern	Sterna sandvicensis									
A	Roseate Tern	Sterna dougallii									
P3/S4	Common Tern	Sterna hirundo									
P4	Arctic Tern	Sterna paradisaea									
A	Sooty Tern	Sterna fuscata									
P5	Little Tern	Sterna albifrons									
P5	Whiskered Tern	Chlidonias hybridus									
A	Black Tern	Chlidonias niger									
A	Razorbill	Alca torda									
A	Puffin	Fratercula arctica									
R1	Rock Dove	Columba livia									
A	Woodpigeon	Columba palumbus									
R3	Bolle´s Pigeon	Columba bollii	CIE								
R4	Laurel Pigeon	Columba junoniae	CIE								
I4	Barbary Dove	Streptopelia risoria									
R2	Collared Dove	Streptopelia decaocto									
S2	Turtle Dove	Streptopelia turtur									
I4	Ring-necked Parakeet	Psittacula krameri									
I4	Monk Parakeet	Myiospsitta monachus									
A	Great Spotted Cuckoo	Clamator glandarius									

STATUS	SPECIES	SCIENTIFIC NAME	Endemic
P4	Cuckoo	Cuculus canorus	
R3	Barn Owl	Tyto alba	
P5	Scops Owl	Otus scops	
A	Tawny Owl	Strix aluco	
R3	Long-eared Owl	Asio otus canariensis	SCCI
W4	Short-eared Owl	Asio flammeus	
A	Nightjar	Caprimulgus europeaus	
R1	Plain Swift	Apus unicolor	ME
P4	Common Swift	Apus apus	
S3	Pallid Swift	Apus pallidus brehmorum	
P4	Alpine Swift	Apus melba	
A	White-rumped Swift	Apus caffer	
A	Little Swift	Apus affinis	
A	Kingfisher	Alcedo atthis	
A	Blue-cheeked Bee-eater	Merops superciliosus	
P4	European Bee-eater	Merops apiaster	
P5	European Roller	Coracias garrulus	
R3	Hoopoe	Upupa epops	
P4	Wryneck	Jynx torquilla	
R3	Great Spotted Woodpecker	Dendrocopos major canariensis	SCCI
A	Bar-tailed Desert Lark	Ammomanes cincturus	
A	Calandra Lark	Melanocorypha calandra	
P4	Short-toed Lark	Calandrella brachydactyla	
R5	Lesser Short-toed Lark	Calandrella rufescens rufescens	SCCI
R4		Calandrella rufescens polatzeki	SCCI
A	Crested Lark	Galerida cristata	
W4	Skylark	Alauda arvensis	
P3	Sand Martin	Riparia riparia	
A	Crag Martin	Ptynoprogne rupestris	
P2	Swallow	Hirundo rustica	
P4	Red-rumped Swallow	Hirundo daurica	
P2	House Martin	Delichon urbica	
A	Richard´s Pipit	Anthus novaeseelandiae	
P3	Tawny Pipit	Anthus campestris	
R1	Berthelot´s Pipit	Anthus berthelotii berthelotii	ME
P3	Tree Pipit	Anthus trivialis	
W4	Meadow Pipit	Anthus pratensis	
P4/W4	Red-throated Pipit	Anthus cervinus	
A	Water Pipit	Anthus spinoletta	
P3	Blue-headed Wagtail	Motacilla (flava) falva	
P3	Yellow Wagtail	Motacilla (flava) flavissima	
R2	Grey Wagtail	Motacilla cinerea canariensis	SCCI
P4/W3	White Wagtail	Motacilla alba	

STATUS	SPECIES	SCIENTIFIC NAME	Endemic								
R2	Robin	Erithacus rubecula superbus	SCCI								
P5	Nightingale	Luscinia megarhynchos									
P5	Bluethroat	Luscinia svecica									
P4/W4	Black Redstart	Phoenicurus ochrurus									
P4	Common Redstart	Phoenicurus phoenicurus									
P4	Whinchat	Saxicola rubetra									
W5	Stonechat	Saxicola torquata									
A	Isabelline Wheatear	Oenanthe isabellina									
P2	Northern Wheatear	Oenanthe oenanthe									
P5	Black-eared Wheatear	Oenanthe hipanica									
A	Desert Wheatear	Oenanthe deserti									
A	Ring Ouzel	Turdus torquatus									
R2	Blackbird	Turdus merula cabrerae	SCM								
A	Fieldfare	Turdus pilaris									
P4/W4	Song Thrush	Turdus philomelos									
W5	Redwing	Turdus iliacus									
A	Mistle Thrush	Turdus viscivorus									
P5	Grasshopper Warbler	Locustella naevia									
P4	Sedge Warbler	Acrocephalus shoenobaenus									
P4	Reed Warbler	Acrocephalus scirpaceus									
P5	Great Reed Warbler	Acrocephalus arundinaceus									
P5	Olivaceous Warbler	Hippolais pallida									
P4	Melodious Warbler	Hippolais polyglotta									
R3	Spectacled Warbler	Sylvia conspicillata orbitalis	SCM								
P4	Subalpine Warbler	Sylvia cantillans									
R3	Sardinian Warbler	S. melanocephala leucogastra	SCCI								
A	Orphean Warbler	Sylvia hortensis									
P5	Common Whitethroat	Sylvia communis									
P4	Garden Warbler	Sylvia borin									
R2	Blackcap	Sylvia atricapilla									
A	Yellow-browed Warbler	Phylloscopus inornatus									
P4	Wood Warbler	Phylloscopus sibilatrix									
P4	Chiffchaff sp.	Phylloscopus sp.									
R1	Canary Islands Chiffchaff	Phylloscopus canariensis	CIE								
P3	Willow Warbler	Phylloscopus trochilus									
R3	Canary Islands Kinglet	Regulus teneriffae	CIE								
P4	Spotted Flycatcher	Muscicapa striata									
A	Red-breasted Flycatcher	Ficedula parva									
P4	Pied Flycatcher	Ficedula hypoleuca									
R2	Blue Tit	Parus caeruleus teneriffae	SCCI								
P4	Golden Oriole	Oriolus oriolus									
A	Red-backed Shrike	Lanius collurio									
R4	Southern Grey Shrike	Lanius meridionalis koenigi	SCCI								
P3	Woodchat Shrike	Lanius senator									

FULL SPECIES CHECKLIST

STATUS	SPECIES	SCIENTIFIC NAME	Endemic								
A	Jackdaw	Corvus monedula									
R4	Raven	Corvus corax tingitanus									
R5/W4	Starling	Strunus vulgaris									
A	Spotless Starling	Sturnus unicolor									
A	Rose-coloured Starling	Sturnus roseus									
I5	Common Myna	Acridotheres tristis									
R1	Spanish Sparrow	Passer hispaniolensis									
R4	Rock Sparrow	Petronia petronia madeirensis	SCM								
R3	Chaffinch	Fringilla coelebs tintillon	SCCI								
R3	Blue Chaffinch	Fringilla teydea teydea	CIE								
R4	Serin	Serinus serinus									
R1	Canary	Serinus canaria	ME								
R3	Greenfinch	Carduelis chloris auantiiventris									
R3	Goldfinch	Carduelis carduelis parva									
W4	Siskin	Carduelis spinus									
R2	Linnet	C. cannabina meadewaldoi	SCCI								
R4	Trumpeter Finch	Bucanetes githagineus amantum	SCCI								
A	Snow Bunting	Plectrophenax nivalis									
A	House Bunting	Emberiza striolata	·								
R3	Corn Bunting	Miliaria calandra									

140

Berthelot's Pipit

nary Islands Kinglet

Blue Chaffinch

Common Chaffinch

Canary

Trumpeter Finch

Bulwer's Petrel

Little Shearwater

Laurel Pigeon

Plain Swift

Bulwer's Petrel

Madeiran Storm-petrel

Little Shearwater

Barbary Falcon

Bolle's Pigeon

Laurel Pigeon

Plain Swift

Berthelot's Pipit

Canary Islands Chiffchaff

Blue Chaffinch

Canary

Trumpeter Finch

BIBLIOGRAPHY

ASHMOLE, M. and P. ASHMOLE. 1989. Natural history excursions in Tenerife: a guide to the countryside, plants and animals. Kidston Mill Press, Scotland.

BANNERMAN, D. A. 1922. The Canary Islands: their history, natural history and scenery. Gurney and Jackson, London and Edinburgh.

BANNERMAN, D.A. 1963. Birds of the Atlantic Islands volume 1: a history of the birds of the Canary Islands and of the Salvages. Oliver and Boyd, Edinburgh and London.

CRAMPS, S et al. 1977-1994. Handbook of the Birds of Europe, the Middle East and North Africa- the birds of the Western Palearctic, volumes 1-9. Oxford University Press, Oxford.

FERNANDEZ, J. M. 1978. Los lepidópteros diurnos de las Islas Canarias. Enciclopedia Canaria. Aula de Cultura de Tenerife.

FERNANDEZ-RUBIO, F. 1991. Guía de Mariposas Diurnas de la Península Ibérica, Baleares, Canarias, Azores y Madeira (2 vols). Pub Pirámide, Madrid.

HEINZEL, H., R. FITTER and J. PARSLOW. 1995. Collins Pocket Guide to Birds of Britain and Europe, with North Africa and the Middle East. 5th Edition. Harper Collins, London.

LORENZO GUITIERREZ, J. A., and J. GONZALEZ DOMINGUEZ. 1993. Las Aves de El Médano. Asociación Tinerfeña de Amigos de la Naturaleza.

MARTIN, A. 1987. Atlas de las Aves Nidificantes en la Isla de Tenerife. Instituto de Estudios Canarios, Tenerife.

MORENO, J. M. 1988. Guía de las Aves de las Islas Canarias. Editorial Interinsular Canaria.

PEREZ PADRON, F. 1986. The birds of the Canary Islands. Enciclopedia Canaria. Aula de Cultura de Tenerife. 3rd edition.

WATSON, L. 1985. Whales of the World – a handbook and field guide to all the living species of whales, dolphins and porpoises. Hutchinson, London.

INDEX TO BIRD SPECIES